Y0-BZY-536

"...do I believe?"

stories and art by survivors

" '...*do I believe?*' stories and art by survivors," by Portland Burn Survivors. ISBN 978-1-62137-424-4.

Library of Congress Control Number: 2014901169.

Published 2014 by Virtualbookworm.com Publishing Inc., P.O. Box 9949, College Station, TX 77842, US. ©2014, Portland Burn Survivors. All rights reserved. No part of this publication may be reproduced, stored in a retrieval system, or transmitted in any form or by any means, electronic, mechanical, recording or otherwise, without the prior written permission of Portland Burn Survivors.

Manufactured in the United States of America.

Thank you Bobsy Graham

Thank you pro photographers: Bendt Sornson, Kevin Rolly, Cat Oshanek, Labonya and Chago. Thanks for the help securing the grant, Mike Yas and Bobsy. Thanks for the laughs and sanity checks Ken and Yogi Rob. Thanks for help editing Kelsey Peake and layout Megan Cavanaugh. Thanks Phoenix Society and Firefighters Quest for being role models. And thank you artists and writers for participating.

Participants:

Rob Bispo
Mona Kreuger
Marty Lupoli
Jamie Uttley
Ibrahim Mubarak
Lisa Fay
Labonya Siddique
Kelly Farladeau
Mark McEachren
Nancy Tran
Carmen Barker
Kenneth G. Alvis
Donna Bailey
Kim Dormier
George Goodwin
Clare Latchem
Yolonda Hawkins
Laura Brixey
Trevor Beam
Sara McIlroy
AnnMarie Balik
Chago Roberto DeSantiago
Bethany Storro
Paul Peterson
Alisa Christensen
Bendt Sornson
Betsy Pucci-Stemple
Chris Baker

Yogi Rob

By Rob Bispo

I was burned on July 25, 2003 by a hot water heater malfunction in the basement of my restaurant. I lost 97% of my skin, the largest organ on our body. As I lit the match I heard a 'Swoosh!' and was ignited; I knew I had one chance to escape. I took a big breath, closed my eyes and headed for the six-foot ladder that led to a hole in the floor. As I started to step on the ladder, a spirit grabbed me. The ladder turned into a stairwell and up I came. I felt this was my mother, who died many years before this accident.

I ran out the back door engulfed in flames, frantically looking for water of any kind, and then heard a loud voice inside my head command "Stop, Drop and Roll!" This refocused me and I put myself out, then ran to the bar a couple businesses down. I burst in and told the bartender to call my Dad, even gave her his number, and said call 911. She did and then told me *to leave her bar.* I couldn't understand why. Later I realized my clothing was burned away and black, charred skin was hanging off of me like ghoulish monster makeup. I know it freaked her out.

I ran back outside and my Dad was pulling up the alley in his Volkswagen; I was relieved to see his face and thought it might be the last time I ever did. As he came running towards me, I noticed my skin melting off of my outstretched arms. "Don't touch me . . ." I said as I passed out.

When I woke up after more than two months in a coma, all I could move were my eyes. I was pissed to say the least. At first I wanted to kill myself but soon realized none of my nurses would help me with that; I needed help with everything. I spent four months in Legacy's burn unit then was transferred to Good Sam's for rehabilitation.

1

Three weeks later, although I was still wheelchair bound and wrapped like a mummy, I was told "you're good to go." Fortunately, my sister is an angel and took me in. I had a home nurse come in the morning every day for a few months to help change bandages. Three times a week a physical therapist came to get me moving. She was a genuinely nice person but still hated having her show up. Physical Therapy was difficult and painful; I forced myself to do it but didn't like the workout.

My doctor told me I would have to stretch and keep stretching for the rest of my life if I wanted to have any quality of life. My mother and my daughter had taught me the healing arts of yoga many years earlier. I didn't know much about yoga, I just remembered it worked and it made me feel better. So I started practicing yoga again to stretch the tight skin grafts that gripped and pinched my body.

After the accident, I spent the next seven years practicing yoga for six to eight hours a day; all of the healing arts. Although I practice them all from time to time, yoga is my passion. Yoga restored my confidence beyond all expectations.

And after you heal yourself you want to help others. As it is with a lot of yoga teachers, it has been a struggle for me. Most of us don't make a whole bunch of money, but we love our work. Things were becoming stagnant in my yoga career. Then I hooked up with Portland Burn Survivors (PBS) and they sponsored a web-page for my practice. It has helped me get farther into the yoga teaching community.

As a burn survivor, I live with chronic pain and I know firsthand what it feels like to be physically weak, painfully inflexible and visibly disfigured.

However, my parents taught me that anything is possible. I teach yoga because I know it can transform your body and restore health, confidence and self-esteem. I am committed to passing on the lessons all of my teachers so generously shared with me. Teaching yoga in Salem is how I share my gratitude for a second chance at life.

It doesn't matter if you are a burn survivor, in a wheelchair, or trying out for the Olympics. I started out at Ground Zero and I'm willing to help anybody rebuild their confidence, self-esteem and strength. Yoga takes care of that void in my soul and makes me feel whole. I have so many friends now I am blessed.

Excerpt from *Sage Was the Perfect Shadow*

By Mona Krueger

My first city, Volgograd (the former Stalingrad), is famous as the setting for one of the definitive battles of World War II. The Russians stopped the Germans at the Volga River by sheer courage and the sacrifice of blood shed. The city remembers its fallen and commemorates them with memorials and designated holidays. One of the traditions for any wedding day is to lay flowers at the eternal flame in honor of the heroes.

I arrived in Volgograd with a group of Americans as a teacher. After perestroika, the time of rebuilding following the fall of communism, we were invited by the ministry of education to do some consulting work in the school system. Fortunately, we worked with interpreters because my initial language skills were nil. I asked one of them to find out if a burn center existed in the city.

My first impression of a Russian hospital was not encouraging. The burn center was overcrowded, dingy, antiquated. A foul smell hit in waves as you entered.

The doctors had skill but limited resources, which meant a person's chances of surviving extensive burns were slim. I received permission to visit patients but found out it was an unusual request. Family and close friends were allowed, but not strangers.

Thus began my knocking on doors, and the reception I received varied. Mistrust was the most common reaction, but if I could prove quickly that I wasn't peddling some cult or pushing a wonder cure, the doors opened.

Being naturally shy, I had to force myself to go every week and risk the potential rejection. I went because I knew the power of camaraderie among burn survivors.

Sonia was a ten-year-old girl brought in from a village clinic. She and her friend, Lena, had thrown a match into an old tank on the orphanage grounds where they lived. It exploded, catching them both on fire.

They didn't even attempt to save Lena, but they took a chance on Sonia. Maybe it was the life in her eyes or the spunky smile she managed, even with burns over 50 percent of her body.

That smile could con a hardened criminal.

And grit was her middle name.

The initial surgeries did not go well, which eventually sealed her fate. Extraordinary measures were not available for a poor, orphaned girl. She had no bribes to give for the specialty bed or the expensive antibiotics.

I watched her deteriorate and tried to be an advocate, helper and big sister, but I didn't understand all that took place behind the scenes. The ward had one Clinitron in a private room, a sand bed that distributes pressure more evenly for wounded skin. Three months into her hospital stay, a new doctor took over and fought to get the bed for her as a last chance effort to save her.

Renewed hope made her fight even harder to live. For whatever reasons, her stint on the bed did not last long. After her next surgery, she woke up in a room with five other patients all crowded together and knew that they were giving up on her. A poem I wrote describes a measure of the trauma:

The Common Room

I remember the way betrayal flashed
out of your deep sad eyes

5

to wake up in a common room
with all hope gone
people chattering around you
in that narrow space
dull lifeless droning ringing in your ears
chanting a death knell

You didn't shed a tear,
but the way you looked at me
those dark pools haunt me still
what could I have done to give you life
incompetent, neglectful, absurd
words that describe your caretakers
those who were supposed to be your advocates
useless all

I was no better
who watches out for such as these
lost children with suffering eyes
the orphans of the world

The bonds of sisterhood
should have been less naive
where was wisdom in that crowded room
you knew they had given up
too many mistakes had been made
failure

How can I tell you my sorrow
the part I played was of one so floundering
I didn't understand the systems in place
I let you down just as they

Too late—much too late
I wish the clock were turned back and
I could have stopped you in that yard

with your friend
lighting that match

You would be a woman now
embracing life instead of death

Sonia lived a grueling seven months.
I have never seen anyone suffer as
she did. Much of the donor skin
sites they had used during the
course of her stay never healed and
these areas became worse than the
original burns.

Her body was half decayed when
she died.

Maybe her death would have been
quicker and less painful if my presence there hadn't spurred the
doctors to try harder. In my attempts to support her, had I only
prolonged her suffering? It was a terrible question that haunted me;
the naive, do-gooder American trying to grasp and influence a
corrupt, flailing medical system.

Sonia had wanted to live so desperately, even on the day they
threatened to cut off her legs.

Her favorite story was of Daniel from the Old Testament. Daniel had
been betrayed and thrown into a pit of lions to be ravaged for his
punishment. God kept him safe through a very long night. Sonia had
been waiting for God's deliverance, too. It didn't come the way she
had hoped, but it came. I pictured her in a better place,

pain-free,
whole,
laughing,
walking with God.

And I had hope that I would see my precious friend again some day.

Marty Lupoli of Salem, Oregon

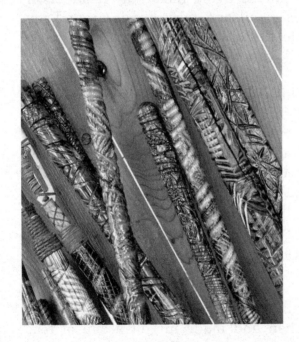

Marty Lupoli carves walking sticks

Autobiography of a Life-Changing Experience

By Jamie Uttley

I pretty much have the life of a mole without any eyes, meaning that my life could take an unsuspecting turn at any moment. I'd just turned seventeen and sighed as I didn't get any joy from birthdays any more. I had been on cannabis for a straight year and enjoyed a drink along with that. Yes, the wicked weed and the dreadful drink. I was troubled with a lot of problems living inside my head. As if Dante himself had wrapped his small and fiery hands around my throat. I was in a vicious circle that racked up debt, made me a piranha to society and most of all, very emotional unstable.

I was constantly locked inside this evil mimic of myself, living under a dirty roof in a town named Higher Blackley. The society there was easy to fit into, as most of the town's citizens were young, drugged and boozed up. Even though I had that opportunity of going out and mingling into that crowd, I mostly chose to stay at home, The Devils Playground. The house was not the best; the wallpaper was hanging off the ceiling and was dark yellow from all the tar from smoking. The place did not smell too great, with the lack of my hygiene combined with it. My days were spent hunting for money for my next fix, until one night.

After seeing my friend off—I had him around to socialize with some cannabis—I went into the kitchen and made myself a cup of tea. During this, I attempted to light a cigarette. All of a sudden a very bright light flashed in front of my eyes, this came with brief and quick warmth. Smelling the singed hairs that were on my body, I realized that it was a gas ignition that lit the room. I patted my torso down as the hairs were still incinerating on my body. In that split second, the fire alarms started ringing. In the corner of my eye,

I saw twinkles of firelight flapping around. I thought to myself, "Something is on fire!"

With adrenaline starting to pump I started to feel this sort of agonizing and burning feeling over my body. With heart pounding and adrenaline at record levels, I quickly ran upstairs to the bathroom and started filling the bath with cold water. With the pain being so unbearable I jumped in straight away. This was a mistake as this made it worse. I sat there in the bath for about at least 30 seconds until I noticed that a big patch of skin on my left arm had peeled away (I would guess it was about 20 cm in length). Looking at my fingers, all of the skin had rolled up. So with the excruciating pain, I jumped out of the bath and ran downstairs and straight out of the door. I was wearing just my boxers.

Hearing the cracks of the kitchen window as I jetted out of the doorway, I collapsed to the floor in shock and pain. Jumping straight back up again, I raced to my neighbor's door and banged so hard the door nearly came off its hinges! No luck, he either was not in or was not answering, as it was two o'clock in the morning. I must have knocked on five doors on my street; I was violently shaking and crunched over as if I had a hunch back because of my freshly cremated skin. Finally someone let me in. I spat my words out at her but she knew what had happened as she had heard my screams of agony. She tried sitting me down, I refused, she tried putting something around me, I refused. Too much pain and shock.

Within minutes, the ambulance arrived. They told me to suck on this equipment they handed to me. I had no idea what it was as it looked like a whistle. Whatever it was, it calmed me down after five minutes. In that space of time, they managed to bandage some of my exposed areas, helped me to a wheelchair and took me to the ambulance. I could see flashing blue lights beaming through the privets in my garden. Once in the ambulance I finally managed to say some words, "How bad are the burns?" I questioned the paramedic. He replied with, "I would say about twenty percent." I was then wondering if he said that to avoid me going into shock even more as the pain felt more than twenty percent! Before I even knew it, I was at Crumpsall Hospital.

The back doors of the ambulance opened as I was faced with the blackness of the sky and some of the patients outside having a smoke. I was covered up in blankets for warmth. The paramedic wheeled me out of the ambulance and left me sitting there outside. I just remember looking at this middle-aged woman as she was looking back at me.

Then I fell into a dream like reality. There was a scenario of me appearing in the television series "Shameless." Now, this was weird as it felt real, like I was there and living the moment. I was experiencing the life of what it would be like in the Chatsworth estate. I faced some of the characters I knew from the show. In another scene, I ended up at some house party in Harpurhey in Manchester. It had an American theme to it, switching scenery to America and then to Harpurhey. I seemed to be there laughing and drinking, my mate was also there who I shared the cannabis with. We were sharing drugs—then that suddenly changed to being arrested in America with drugs.

That quickly changed to me being up where my dad's family lives. I know it's a horrible place but I was with my family and as it is up in the hills, I found myself feeling really cold. I knew my dad liked going fishing so I dreamed I was hacking ice with a ball and chain to try and find a fishing spot. I was hearing faint voices of people talking to me within this scenario. There was this last scene I recall being back in the late 1920's. I had the strange feeling that I was stuck in that era but I knew I was living in the year 2012.

I was walking on cobbled streets as horse carts trotted by. I was then in some sort of old house, where people were talking to me, having real life-like conversations. This made me paranoid so I ran as far away as I could from that house. I ended up in some church with a beast looking down upon me. He was making me levitate towards him. I was struggling to try to set myself free. Everything started to get blurry and then the beast spoke, "I will get you next time."

These bizarre scenes must seem to you as dreams but for me they were reality.

I slowly opened my eyes and found myself in a hospital room with my father looking down at me. "Hey Jimbob," he greeted. I was still nauseous about the visions I just had. After getting used to my surroundings and knowing this was real and my dad was real, I tried to talk. I could not speak a word. Seems I'd had a tracheotomy. This was truly shocking news. I tried to move, it was useless. I was paralyzed to this hard, uncomfortable hospital bed. I looked down upon my body to see that I had been bandaged up, head to toe. At this point my head was spinning and my eyes filled with tears; I could not move or speak. I was worried that I could be like this forever.

I had three blood tubes in my veins. One in the side of my right leg, one in my left hand and one in my right arm. Furthermore, I was given a catheter for my urine. This was hell! Then Dad tells me that I had been asleep for three whole weeks. *This is great news*, I thought whilst having a frowned face. He was telling me that my Mum had been in every day to see me—she is a saint! And that my aunties have been in to see me. This probably explains the mad dreams I was having in Bacup. The "Shameless" one I can explain clearly as I loved watching that program. The American one, well I have not got one single idea on that.

I cannot remember the rest of the events for that day. From day one being in the Intensive Care Unit, nights were the worst for me. They slowly got worse as the nurses gradually stopped sedating me. I slept most of the time. I remember a few nights where the doctors came in to move me around and change positions so I did not acquire bed sores. The nights were also bad in the sense of me being still under the influence of medication. The room didn't appear as it seemed at all. The roof was black and it was always dark with a little light in the middle. Other patients rolled past me with their nurses pushing their beds. They stared at me and I felt rather uncomfortable.

I can always remember and cherish the days when my Mum came in. She cried a lot when she saw me and how well I was coming on each day. One day she massaged cream into my hands as I was plastered with dead skin. This sent me to sleep every time. Another day there was a little moment we had when she was holding my hand and I was lip speaking, "I love you." Mum fully understood and said it

straight back to me and wept. She was happy that I was there and improving each day.

Each day resembled an even bigger step I took. Half way through my journey in the ICU, I had my catheters removed. This was so relieving but irritable because my bowels were prone to relaxation. This is why I couldn't move and I realized that in the end as a physiologist came in and gave my skin a stretch everyday. She told me why she was doing it and how I couldn't move. As every day went by, the room looked more real and I started to realize what things were as the sedation slowly left my system.

The next big step was that the nurses gave me an item to go with my tracheotomy. This enabled me to talk very faintly and croaky for the first time. This was an amazing feeling because I was always a really chatty person. I started to talk to my Dad and my Mum about how upset I was and what had really happened. I talked to them for hours. More to my Mum really as I knew how much effort she had put in for me. I felt happy as I knew that I still had my family to count on for support.

The worst experience I endured throughout the hospital stay was the bandage changes. This was very distressing and had to happen every two days. I used to bleed as the nurses ripped off the bandages that were soaked with this special cream. This was really painful as my skin was still severely burnt. It was also the time where I could see my injuries in the real state, with blood oozing out of the worst parts.

A great experience was when the physiologist came in one day and confidently said, "Right, we are going try and stand up to today." This is because she knew how far I was coming along on getting my strength back. I could not eat or drink yet and I was still on a drip. This was a bonus for my skin repair in my opinion. Along with her assistant, they wheeled in some sort of queer object. They explained to me what it was. It was a winch to help me stand up onto my feet for the very first time! My Mum was here to witness this remarkable event, and it pulled through smoothly and I managed to step up onto my feet before I got winched back down into a wheelchair. I was wheeled outside with my mum where I took my first breath of life again. This is where my Mum's sister met me for a surprise visit.

For the last part of my journey throughout the ICU, I embarked on an enlightening voyage through remorse and epiphanies. I felt stronger towards my family and I knew that I did not need weed any longer. I had my blood tubes taken out of my veins and I was put on portable oxygen. Then I was transferred out of the ICU and into my very own ward. I was still on the drip and had blood taken regularly, but it was still a massive step. I achieved the greatest feeling with the slight change of scenery and I gathered knowledge of actually where I was from a nurse name Claire. I was situated at Wythenshaw hospital in the burns unit.

The first night of being in my ward was a tricky one as I was up all night in pain. I had to sleep on this special, blow up mattress custom made for my requirements. For a good few weeks I woke up every hour on the hour in pain and I would have to take some more doses of morphine. I also had a lot of this for bandage changes too. I had a window in my room so it was not all that bad. There was a bathroom sink, my own portable table on wheels, a wardrobe, a set of drawers and a mirror. But it was not exactly paradise being in that room every day.

An ENT (ear, nose and throat) doctor inspected me a few times along with the physiotherapist. They noticed I was coming on rather well; my Mum and the family were kept up to date with this too. I was soon on thickened liquids. After a month of not drinking, this was heaven to me! I started to look on the bright side then; on that same day my tracheotomy tube had been taken out. My voice was starting to sound stronger each week.

A few more weeks down the line I could walk to the bathroom and back. I was really out of breath a lot when I walked that far, so I had regular blood pressure and heart rate checks. But still, this was a great accomplishment from when I was in the ICU unit a month ago.

I started having conversations with the staff in the burns unit and my Mum and Dad. They all said I was coming along very well. Now that I had my tracheotomy out, my catheters out and my voice was starting to get back to normal, the next step was me to get off the drip and start eating. I was taken down to the café in a wheelchair by my dad. Every time I did this, I tried walking towards the café; it was a bit of a long way. I managed to get further each time we went until I was fit enough to walk all the way. Another great accomplishment; the family was over the moon.

I had started to notice that my burns were healing very well. They had turned out to be seventy percent burns instead of twenty percent. The staff said I would have been in the hospital for a year but now they begged to differ. I still have the same face as I used to have; I have changed life towards a happier and brighter future.

Two months out of the ICU and I was able to put my DVDs in my own portable DVD player, get coffees from the café, go on walks and all the general things I have to do in life. It's going all uphill for me. After solid physical therapy everyday, I have noticed that my skin has become slacker and it is beginning to get easier to move, but I am still all in bandages though. It turns out that the next week the nurses say they are putting less bandages on my chest area as parts of it has healed up. This was great news to hear. My family was thrilled to bits when they heard this. They came in once every two days.

A bad experience was waking up at eight o'clock in the morning to take medications, which made me disorientated for the day. It was bad enough as every night I did not sleep well at all. I would say this along with changing my bandages would have been the very worst of the journey, despite the ICU treatment.

On the brighter side I was happy because I could see that my burns were slowly getting better. The nurses came in a told me some great news each week and I had a mass of family support. I constantly had the thought of, *I was getting out soon.* I forgot how many times I used to cry each day. I was really excited, upset and then depressed, so I had very mixed emotions each day. I treated every day as another piece to my story.

So, it got to three months out of ICU and I was preparing for my first home visit. I was enthusiastic and anxious. It was so long since I had stayed at my mother's house. It was about ten in the morning and I was still waking up after the prepared breakfast I'd just finished. My Mum was picking me up at one o'clock in the afternoon. I was counting down the minutes! I tried to play on my Nintendo dual screen to take my mind off things. Looking back at the clock it was quarter to one. I thought I would go for a cigarette before my mother came. I walked outside into the burns unit's garden and lit up.

I felt a tap on my shoulder and I turned around to see it was my Auntie. She said that were here and ready to take me home for the night. Then my Mother came strolling in; we all had a cigarette together and talked about our mornings. Before I knew it I was in the car and on the way home for the first time in a while.

Once at my Mother's home I started to explore. I had not seen inside this home for quite some time so I had to get to know my surroundings again. The night progressed on and I was tired by eight o'clock. So, I went straight to bed, slept right through the night and woke up the next morning feeling quite great. *It was the best sleep I'd had in ages*, I thought to myself. My Auntie soon showed up to take me back to hospital. This is when it got more interesting.

We showed up at the burns unit and the nurse approached us. We halted in our position. Me, my Mum and my Auntie all looked at this nurse. "We have some good news; it looks like after the weekend we will be looking at discharging you from hospital. This is because you are doing so well and there is no need to bandage you up any more as your burns are all healed." We were all shocked by the news and hugged each other. Trying to take in the news still, we spoke to the nurse on how well I was during the home visit.

My Mum and Auntie left after talking to the nurse. All I had to do now is get through the weekend. This was pretty easily done as I had a bit of pain, was not taking as many pills and was having better sleeps. Before I knew it, it was the following Monday. I finished my physiology session and the physician gave me an appointment card to come back later in the week for another assessment. My Mum arrived with my Auntie again. I had the most amazing feeling ever as I knew I would be walking out of this wretched place of bad memories and being set free to a brighter and fresh new start to life. The nurses prescribed me some medications I had to take and some extra pads for my sensitive parts of skin.

I was good to go! I took the steps of courage out of the hospital and felt the fresh air slap against my face and creep up my nostrils. This was the most exiting experience of my life. I felt like the ball and chain had been taken off and I could breathe normally and have my free will again, quitting the drugs and alcohol. How could the second chance that God gave me go bad?

From the day I got out of hospital up until today, I feel like a new man. I do not have the urge to take drugs or alcohol. I have an amazing girlfriend and feel as if I am more confident and special. The feelings of depression and anxiety have slowly left my system and I have nearly finished my road to recovery. This year of 2012 has been very tough and frightening. On the other hand, I do not look back on this as I have grown stronger and look forward to my future and the fresh start at life I was given.

A door opens and I look away to hide my eyes so I do not see being seen.
Chago Roberto DeSantiago

Leaving My Youth Behind

By Lisa Fay

It was the summer of my fifteenth year, and this year was to be a new start in a new city. Just weeks before, I had left the familiar northeastern city and my family and friends for the desert southwest. Strange, unfamiliar and dreadfully hot, I met some new people and soon after they invited me to join them at a lake not too far from the city. Of course, at fifteen I wanted to have something new and different to do, so I said yes! Little did I know my life would be altered from this casual trip to the lake.

We set off on Friday and within an hour, we were there setting up fishing poles, catching a fairly good bounty of perch and bluegill for what would later be dinner. The afternoon sun was baking my fair eastern skin leaving it very red. As the day went on we drank, sang to the radio, laughed and did many other things. Life and times with this new group of friends was fun. I used to say "cool" a lot back then. Evening approached and a fire was started for the cooking of the fish. I was happy to do my part in helping any way I could. I wanted to feel useful and like I belonged. Dinner was good and the drinks continued to flow; others who were along the shoreline joined us from time to time. For me, the trip to the lake was going great and I was happy to be able to partake in this desert ritual with my new friends.

Night fall came and the fire has increased to a giant Bonfire! The drinks and other indulgences were still going around and the Hell's Angels were firing guns from the hillside above us toward the water. This was not a good time for a swim! People were still wandering from camp circle to camp circle but I was now getting chilled. I decided to lay down in a lawn chair and put on some nylon legging, wrapping myself up in a blanket and watching everyone having a good time. It wasn't long before I was out. Sometime after, a guy who had been creating mischief throughout the day came over. He was still at it and was asked to leave. He left, leaving behind an unopened can of beer for our bonfire. The can exploded, fire, embers, wood and pieces of the can went flying everywhere including all over me. I awoke screaming as my legs were on FIRE. The sheer pain was surreal. Nothing could have prepared me for this.

My newfound friends grabbed me and ran me to the water tossing me like a rag doll into the lake. My clothing was melting to my legs where the flames burned down into the flesh. The pain was so intense that there was ringing in my ears and flashes of light appeared like a strobe light in my eyes. After the shock of the cold water and the fact that I had to come up for air to breath, I saw everyone on a frenzy to contain the situation. The Hell's Angels, who were partying above us, were chasing down the guy who threw the can into our fire. The camps that partied all day by us were trying to contain the fire and make sure no one else was hurt. In the chaos someone shouted, "We need to get her to the hospital." I was adamant that was not going to happen! My mother could never know what took place and with who that night.

It was excruciating peeling the nylon from the gaping wounds that speckled my thighs. I cried countless tears and drank a lot that night to try to alleviate the pain that was encompassing my being. I'm not sure if I had enough or the new friends and people surrounding me thought they could do no more to patch me up, but I passed out. They told me before I did, I stressed no hospital! In excruciating, relentless pain and suffering, I insisted we party on through Saturday and Sunday. Through many pleas to go back and pain shouting from what seemed to be everywhere on me, we stayed. I would look at and clean my wounds every couple of hours and dress them the best that could be done from the middle of nowhere. There was no way I wanted to explain what was going on with me to my mother.

Although my excitement and happy times ended on Friday night with the igniting of my flesh, the parties lasted until Sunday night when we packed up and headed back to the city. Here the real test of my strength started; I was terrified of my mother and her evil ways and felt the cover up had to begin. I stopped wearing short shorts, skirts and bathing suits. I made sure she was not around when I showered or cared for my wounds. Buying the bandages and the antibiotic ointment was not an issue; I had already established an income for myself at a pretty good rate. The pain continued for months as I had to hide the wounds and clothes were rubbing my skin and ripping the tissue away. I failed gym class that year for not changing. That's okay, I was dealing with a lot of emotional baggage from that night and Gym wasn't a big deal.

I had nightmares for years afterward and the idea of wearing a bathing suit was a definite No! It's over thirty years later and the events of that night still have lasting effects on the way I look at myself and the way I allow others to be in my space. Relationships are still a challenge for me, because I tend to be very closed off and keep up barriers. These barriers hide pain, disappointment, vulnerability and layers of emotional scars. The scars, both physical and mental, have many distinct layers and all have a story that follows.

Lisa Fay and Ibrahim Mubarak

Spotted Foot

By Ibrahim Mubarak

I can remember the moment well and I'm often reminded of the incident each time I put on my socks or wash my foot.

It was a normal, cold winter day in Chicago. We as children often imitate our favorite sports team and on that team we play like the players that catch our attention. Chicago has plenty of Sports teams. The Chicago Cubs and White Socks were our Baseball teams, The Chicago Bulls our Basketball team, the Chicago Bears football and the Chicago Black Hawks our hockey team.

We were playing hockey on a frozen pond. I grew up in the poor area of Chicago where we didn't have an ice rink, so the pond was sufficient. I, with my ruff style and aggressive play was often on a defensive position after my favorite player, Keith Magenson. Yes, Hockey is a popular sport in the African Community and despite popular belief we did play hockey on ice skates and roller skates inside the gym.

On the day it happened, we had been playing for about three hours, skating and playing really hard, to have something to do and to stay warm. After we finished I was so cold that I decided to walk home with my ice skates on. As I walked into the house, I noticed that my older brother had a hot pan of grease and was attempting to fry a plate of french fries. I took my skates off and went into the kitchen just as he was putting a handful of potatoes in the hot skillet that had been sitting in water. When the water from the potatoes hit the hot grease, it splattered on his hand and as he jerked away from the steam, he hit the handle of the skillet and knocked it onto my foot.

Now that was pain and all I could think to do was run. My brother and I were both screaming. My mother ran down the stairs and couldn't really understand what was going on, so she reacted and pulled my sock off and I saw my skin bubbling. My brother was in so much shock that he fainted. I was concerned with what had happened to my brother and my poor mother didn't know who to attend to first. In all the confusion, my mother grabbed a container of uncooked lard and started putting it on my foot; she said that it would draw the heat but heat was all I could feel.

After four months of treatments back and forth to the doctor, my foot never did regain its color back. It still looks all spotted. For years I wouldn't let anyone see my foot. All through high school and college I used to sleep with my socks on. I even made love with my socks on. I don't remember when I started sleeping with my socks off or making love without my comfort of socks. However, as I write this story, I still realize the effect of that day and its impression on me and my life style. The Spotted Foot!

As a child, I used to dream about growing up to be the most beautiful woman in the world.
Dream about being a star; a model or an actress.
Labonya Siddique

At age 8yrs, on 11th May 2000 in Dhaka Bangladesh, I suffered from a Kerosene lantern
explosion during a black out.
Labonya Siddique

The Ugly Scar-Faced Girl

By Kelly Falardeau

When I was only two years old I lived on a farm. My cousins were visiting for the weekend and our grandfather asked them to burn the shingles from the old barn roof.

I went by the fire to watch my cousins throw the shingles. Mike and Rod were eleven and nine respectively. I was on one side of the burning barrel; a spark landed on my dress and when I came around to the other side I was engulfed in flames. Our neighbor was driving down the driveway, saw me in flames and grabbed the bucket of water and threw it on me to put out the fire.

My mom heard all the crying and screaming from inside the house and ran outside only to see me engulfed in flames.

All the way to the hospital, my mom could hear me crying and saying *"Mommy, it hurts, please take the pain away."* There was nothing she could do as she cried herself. She was only 21 years old, barefoot and seven months pregnant.

When we got to the hospital, the doctors and nurses were waiting for me; they grabbed me from my mom's arms and took me to the operating room. They knew I was in a life or death situation; time was precious and every minute was crucial for my survival.

They needed to get a tracheotomy into me so I would be able to breathe when the swelling took over. I didn't look like the cute little two year old girl that my parents once knew me as. I was now scarred for life if I even survived. The chances of me surviving were slim to none.

My grandpa went to see our pastor at the church because he felt tremendous guilt for asking his grandsons to burn the shingles. How could he be so stupid to ask kids to burn stuff in a fire? The pastor told him there was a reason I got burned and I would live. 'There had to be some reason why this precious two year old got burned, she has a purpose in this world. God will not let her die.' At one point, I did die and the doctors brought me back to life.

I spent three months in the hospital and two days a week they would take me into the operating room and do any procedures that needed to be done. Although I don't remember my accident or my surgeries before I was five years old I do remember the operating room.

I remember being totally scared and the nurses telling me I had to get naked and put on the hospital gown. One time I kept my panties on underneath the hospital gown, secretly hoping the nurse wouldn't notice, but she did and told me I had to take them off. I felt completely bare and insecure even with the hospital gown on. I hated being naked.

I would be laying on my hospital bed waiting for the strange man (porter) to come and wheel me to the operating room. And I would be so scared because my mom and dad couldn't be with me and I would have to be taken to the strange places (operating room) in the hospital where again I would be seeing more strange people (more doctors and nurses) and smells. The operating rooms were usually down long, dimly lit hallways in the basement with even more strange smells.

The people I saw were faceless, all covered in ugly green gowns with caps and masks and rubber gloves on. They would talk to me but I could hardly hear them because of the masks they were wearing, plus I was half deaf. All I could see were their eyes. I had to trust them that they were going to do the right thing to me and not take me to some evil place away from my family. I remember the anesthesiologist using the gas mask to put me to sleep and the smell of it and how much I hated it, it would create a sense of panic.

Imagine being two, laying on a stretcher with a bright light above your head and strangers dressed in ugly green hospital gowns

wearing masks, caps and rubber gloves all rushing around the room getting the room ready for my surgery. I remember a nurse holding my hand and saying to me, *"Do you need anything, is there anything I can do for you?"* And answering, *"I need water."* The only water she could give me was a wet face cloth. She would squeeze the water into my mouth; it was never enough, but it was the best she could do. The next thing I remember is the anesthesiologist telling me who he was and that he would be putting a mask over my face to put me to sleep and for me to count to ten.

I had to go through the surgeries every two years because I needed to grow, giving my doctor more skin to work with. My last appointment was when I was nineteen and my doctor told me that there was nothing more he could do for me. There was no other surgery he could do to make my scars disappear forever. I would have to learn to live with the way I looked, still covered in ugly scars. I was done and my only options were to wear make-up and long sleeves so nobody could see my ugly scars. I was devastated; as far as I was concerned he hadn't done enough to take my scars away. I was still ugly, not beautiful like I wanted to be.

How did I handle all the staring, teasing and rejection? It certainly wasn't easy; I dealt with it every day. I remember when I was seventeen and praying at night. "Dear God, please don't make me wake up in the morning, but if I have to, can I at least be scar-less and pretty like all the other girls. Pleeeeeeeeease, thank you, amen."

When I was eighteen I went through a time when I wanted to know 'why' I lived. The odds of a two year old surviving third degree burns to 75% of her body in 1968 were extremely slim. I thought hypnosis might answer that question. I discovered that God gave me a choice to live or die and I chose to live because he said I was too young to die, I had a whole life ahead of me.

Even though I was known as the 'ugly scar-faced girl' in school, I ended up getting married, having three beautiful kids (and a stillborn). Most recently, I was honored by Queen Elizabeth with the Diamond Jubilee medal plus the YWCA honored me with a Woman of Distinction award for my work as an inspirational speaker and three-time best selling author. Yes, I did have a full life ahead of me with a purpose.

Jesus Is a Blue Flame

By Mark McEcham

When I first moved to LA, I worked one day at a Christmas tree lot. There were several reasons why I didn't continue, foremost being that I don't like getting dirty, but the other was that the Lot Manager believed in managing by duress and ridicule.

You know the type . . . they are decent, hardworking men but feel they have to test to see if you have the 'Measure of a Man.' (I just wanted to do the work . . . not pass the test.)

During my one day stint, I met this very cool kid in his early 20's. We had an unspoken respect for one another the moment we met. He understood my discomfort with this manager and immediately looked to shield and protect me and show me the ropes. He taught me how to tie a tree onto a car roof.

To this day I cannot remember his name but I remember being very impressed with his character and integrity. He was good looking, long, lean, dark hair, had a causal demeanor and a genuine smile. He told me about his girlfriend, his future plans of work and school and his strong faith in Christ (this was most impressive).

He truly believed in helping *and* caring for people (unusual in today's youth, right?).

I remember thinking, *I really like this guy, we are sure to be long term friends.*

The next morning, the more I thought about duress & ridicule, the more anxious I felt, so I opted to leave that situation. I went to the lot and returned my new work gloves and tree trimmers. I didn't get to see the kid again or say goodbye. About three months later, I was sitting in a coffee shop reading the paper and in walks the kid. Same good looks, same genuine smile and same demeanor of care. We talked for a while and we both agreed that we needed to see each other again. But (of course) we did not exchange information; time goes by and moves on.

I started work at Sevilla and my life moved into different orbits and cycles. I read the paper everyday; there was a two or three day story that I found to be disturbing, moving and oddly curious.

There are many remote areas in the hills of Santa Barbara and surrounding areas. These back country regions provide havens for communal people, earthy types and general escapists. That's cool . . . sometimes I seek the same solace. The story was about one of these rural homes that had been rented to a young man and his dog. For some reason (later to be discovered) there had been an explosion. It happened in the afternoon while the young man was sleeping. The story described how the man had dove out a window after the explosion had happened.

He was burned (severely) on more than 70% of his body; after diving out the window he was totally disoriented. He wandered up a trail to a field some half-mile away. All the while his dog followed *closely* behind staying by his side the entire time. He was found an hour later and rushed to the hospital in critical condition.

There were several follow up stories speculating attempted suicide (with a propane tank?) to irregularities in housing standards and regulations. It turned out the owners were at fault and legal actions were to ensue. They talked a bit about the young man's condition (but more about the dog). I remember finding it sad how little was said about this man after day three or four . . . I also remember feeling really disturbed about how abrupt that explosion experience must have been for him. (I mean . . . he was asleep).

About three months ago I was sitting in the same coffee shop . . . and in walks the kid . . . *again*. He had the same genuine smile (there was no mistaking that) but I have to say it took me a good minute or two to register who that smile belonged to.

The scars of his reality were apparent. His nose and ears were reconstructed (gone). His fingers had basically melted away and skin graphs could be seen on any flesh that was visible (a horrible sight). It took me a minute to register the character . . . another minute or two to adjust to the visual.

He was amazingly affable (I was incredibly uncomfortable). I asked him to sit down. We began with a few minutes of space filling small talk and catch up conversation. Mine about Sevilla and such. All the while, my mind was spinning because I was looking (and trying not to look) at his destroyed body and face. I thought to myself, *do I just ask what happened? Do I simply act as if it isn't an issue?*

I felt stupid, awkward . . . and oddly removed. It was just awful. *He was* such a good looking kid! After sputtering my space filling stuff, the conversation came to his past six months. He went right into the explosion experience. I was amazed. I told him I had read the story (all of them) and had absorbed  every detail. *It was him.* I still have a hard time wrapping my mind around this. *It was him.*

The afternoon of the explosion, he was laying in bed napping. He woke up to a feeling that there was someone in his house. He stood up and saw a wall of flame coming directly at him.

In that exact moment he uttered, "Jesus!" Because the fire was upon him, the word he uttered came out in a blue flame. He was breathing and speaking fire.

I listened to him speak and my body went weak. Again, I was dumfounded, awkward and so uneasy that I simply did not know what to say or do. It's weird but I *couldn't* be consoling or cool when so uncomfortable. I simply told him that I was glad to see that he had recovered so well, that we must get together (although I work a lot) and I'll see him. And there I went, feeling like a disoriented coward, as I fled his obvious loneliness and my fear of his realities.

The rest of that day I just could not believe how deeply affected I was by this all. Him, me, life, actuality, reality. That night at work I told everyone the story. We all seemed to react somewhat the same way. Dismayed, saddened, fearful. I thought of him a lot.

I recently did some work with a very cool female photographer in downtown Los Angeles named Alisa. We had talked over the phone several times prior to our meeting. She had explained to me how she was in an accident and therefore, walked with a cane (I figured a car accident).

She was wonderful . . . such character! She used to be a stunt woman! It turns out her accident was a camping accident. She had bought a new thermo sleeping bag for the trip. Somehow, it caught fire when she was in it and she was severely burnt on her feet, and it destroyed most of her right arm and hand. She was in intensive care for months. While recovering she had a stroke which resulted in more months in intensive care.

She said the most disturbing thing about the stroke was she could no longer string her thoughts together. That she would forget whole episodes of her life. That if a Dick & Jane book were placed before her she simply couldn't figure out what it said (although she knew she should know).

Her life changed so dramatically and quickly, I was dumbfounded, again! Here's what got me the most: we were driving in her car back to mine and talking about her life, her experiences, and her future and she said, "you know Mark, all of this physical stuff is bad enough but the worst thing is, most of my friends have left."

I thought about it and said (in my dumbfounded swirl), "well I'm sure your TRUE friends have stayed by your side."

"No I was a good judge of character, they *were* good friends. They left because no one wants to be near, or reminded of, Frankenstein." I shivered because I thought about how beautiful she was, then I thought of the kid, and no matter how much I hated that *Awful Truth*, spoken so matter of factly, almost eloquently from Alisa . . . it was true.

I didn't know how to be near it. I didn't want to be near it. I couldn't be near it.

It. Isn't that awful? I mean them.

And if I did stay near them, say out of guilt, it would be contrived, forced, and even more uncomfortable for everyone. Here's the kicker . . . three days ago I was at Trader Joe's buying my dinner for the night. I had just finished working out, my mind was full of silly little life worries that don't really amount to much of anything. I walk out the door with my arms full of groceries and who do I run into? You've got it . . . the kid.

I say, "Hey . . . what are you doing?"

"Well," he says, still smiling (but all genuine essence gone), "I'm homeless."

I'm shocked and say, "Aren't they taking care of you? What about the lawsuit? The Settlement?"

"Yeah, it's all in the works." He went on and on about many different babbling things (I couldn't register any of it). I was shocked, stunned and numb by all the implications of that moment . . . he had *literally* gone crazy. It was evident his mind was gone. I believe he was on drugs as well.

I gave him what money I had on me, looked him in the eyes deeply (with a little less cowardess in my demeanor) and told him what a beautiful person I had always thought him to be, and said goodbye.

I went to my car, closed the door, turned on the engine, turned off the radio and cried.

Who I cried for I honestly can't tell you. I'm still working that out.

Actuality and Reality.

I wish I had hugged him.

But I couldn't.

Marty Lupoli

A Nod of Recognition

By Mona Krueger

Attitude is everything
Not to exude sunshine in some fake way
But to face issues head on
Transparency
Painstaking honesty
It draws the other in
Forges companionship
Camaraderie
To listen with our hearts
The underlying story
Nuances sequestered in words
Meaning creeping forward
Behaviors understood
The whys at times mystery
But life unfolds all the same
And with it
A cry for compassion
Understanding
Relating to the human condition
A nod of recognition
That we are strugglers all

Nancy Tran

Twelve years ago at the age of nineteen, I was doused with gasoline in my sleep. Never would I have thought I would ever be in this position. I met him when I was fifteen years old at a friend's birthday party. He was nineteen at the time. When I was introduced to him, I instantly had a gut feeling that hit me at the pit of my stomach but I didn't know why, so I ignored it. I also thought he was much too old for me to date, but again I was a young girl who dreamt of being in love like a princess. Two weeks later he asked me out. I thought it was moving too fast, but again I ignored it. I didn't want to hurt his feelings. Our relationship consisted of phone calls since I had a strict father who was overprotective. We would talk every day, then I noticed it was every other day and then it stopped ringing. He disappeared without an explanation. I later found out he was doing drugs, so I reached out to him hoping I could help him. Our relationship rekindled.

Throughout our relationship, he disappeared on and off quite frequently without any explanations. I was sick and tired of it and realized a real man would not do that, but somehow he always managed to win me back. He was manipulative, charming and always knew the right things to say to me. I was always crying, emotional and no longer the happy-go-lucky girl I used to be before I met him. At the age of eighteen, I realized he was not the guy I wanted to marry but I did not know how to break up with him then.

His family was very different than mine. I saw a dysfunctional family who didn't know how to express love and support for their children. He was jealous of my upbringing, my family and the support system that I had. We started to argue a lot. My feelings were diminishing, yet something inside me was fearful of breaking up with him. Keep in mind, throughout the course of our relationship, he never hit me, shoved me, pinched, or anything physical for that matter. He called me "useless" once and it hurt my feelings to the core. Although it hurt me, I knew this would be the perfect opportunity to break up, but when I did, he somehow made me feel that I needed to save him again. I lost that battle. My family and friends were disapproving our relationship and in my mind, I thought my family was just saying that so that I would stay home more often. I thought, *Well, they don't know him the way I know him.*

Nancy Tran (fourth from the left) and friends

As our relationship progressed, it was easier to break up and get back together. On my final last break up, I was actually serious about it and he knew it. He said to me, "I'll see you on the other side." In my mind I thought he was suicidal and was concerned about him. Months went by and I made some arrangements where I would go to school in San Francisco and start anew. After my trip back from apartment searching and checking out the campus, he contacted me for one last dinner. My gut feeling told me not to go alone and I said, "If only we can have some other people there too." He agreed. During our dinner I noticed he was sad, but I ignored it. I was tired of his acting and was ecstatic that I felt free and was moving forward. After dinner, my friends parted ways and the ex wanted to take me home. I figured, *Why not, it's his last time anyway.* He gave me a hug, dropped me off and I got ready to go bed.

My three-year-old little cousin wanted to sleep with me, so I snuggled up with him fell asleep. At 4:30 in the morning, I woke up in flames and realized it was not a nightmare. It was real. I was put out; there was an angel watching out for my cousin, because he was against the wall and not burned. My aunt who put me out with a blanket pulled me close to her and said, "You smell like gasoline!

Why do you smell like gasoline?!" I initially thought it was an electrical house fire but no one in the house was burned but me. That was when I knew it was the ex.

I never saw it coming. Again, throughout our relationship he never hit me, pushed me, or called me names continuously. All I had were my instincts, yet I ignored them. I would just keep on going to find evidence just to prove my instincts wrong only to be hurt at the end. (He is now in prison).

Today I am 32 years old and living life to the fullest. The incident has been a blessing in disguise as I was able to find my passion in life: to help veterans returning home from combat who are suffering from post-traumatic stress disorder, amputees, physical ailment, disfigurement and burns. My goal is to assist their transition back with normalcy due to their traumatic changes. Although my incident was caused by an ex-boyfriend here in the United States, I feel a connection and passion to take care of our troops and service members who have taken care of our country and have taken a risk from their lives to protect ours. I am currently going to school at University of Southern California, concentrating in mental health and sub-concentrating in military social work.

My words of advice are to listen to your inner voice and follow your heart. Don't wait until it's too late. Be with someone who brings out the best in you, not the worst. Live your life to the fullest and do not let fear or anyone imprison you from your dreams.

I Believe

By Carmen Barker

Do I believe?
After looking different from one day to another
And feeling shoved away?
. . . I Believe.
Do I believe?
After being separated from my son
And only being able to see him for a tiny bit?
. . . I believe.
Do I believe?
Despite going through endless crying days and nights
And with a sense of loss of everything?
. . . I believe.
Do I believe?
Despite going through adjusting to a completely new life
Along with a painful surgery routine?
. . . I believe.
Do I believe?
Even though I look horrible and swollen right after surgeries
And having to deal with adjusting again and depression?
. . . I believe.
Do I believe?
After feeling lonely, ugly, rejected,
And along with all the stares?
. . . I believe.
Do I believe?
When my baby tells me he loves me
And that I'm still his mommy no matter what I look like?
. . . Yes, I believe.
Do I believe?
When my beautiful families and friends are there for me

And we're building a closer bond?
. . . Yes, I believe.
Do I believe?
When I'm receiving awesome work and care
From my doctors and nurses whom I trust and love?
. . . Yes, I believe.
Do I believe?
When I'm a part of the burn SURVIVOR community
Full of resilience, motivation and Inspiration?
. . . Yes, I believe.
Do I believe?
When I'm blessed with a yearly trip to the World Burn Congress
Where I get to meet up with my burn SURVIVOR family from across
the world?
. . . Oh yes! I believe.
Do I believe?
When I'm finally being loved for who I really am
Despite of all my visual scars?
. . . Oh yes! I believe.
Do I believe?
That I am beautiful, smart, worthy and strong way over the top
And WILL accomplish my goals?
. . . Oh yes dear lord! I believe!
Do I believe?
That God is faithful and will never abandon me?
That he will teach me and guide me everywhere I go
And that he loves me unconditionally?
. . . Oh yes, I BELIEVE
and it is why I have all along.

~This poem shows how I never lost my faith and never gave up. I'm
still working hard to make a home for my son and I, hoping that one
day soon we'll finally be together again.

Carmen Barker before

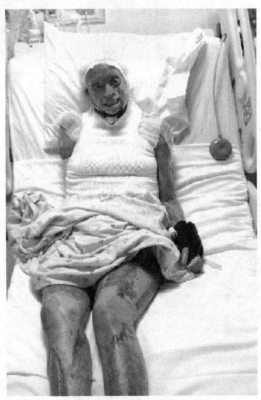

Carmen Barker after

Intro to Silver Works

By Kenneth Alvis

These pieces were created using what is known as the "lost wax" technique. Many modern strategies are now employed in the process of creating "invested" pieces for adornment. The steps used remain remarkably similar to the steps gleaned from craftsmen and cultures throughout past centuries. I found carving the wax (Step

1) to form an enjoyable, sublime experience. My vision easily transferred into the wax block. Maybe not easily . . . exactly. Enough to stay fun.

Mounting the finished wax carving on the "sprue base" is, I find, to be the most tedious, trying step in the whole process. The piece, or pieces, must be placed and spaced to allow even, smooth flow of the molten metal. Anything you screw up here will be mirrored in the final art piece.

The spruce base is married to the investment flask. This part used to freak me out a bit, but I kind of have that part down, most days. Check to make sure everything is still in place.

Investment flask and proudly carved, strategically sprue base mounted wax models are then covered with a pancake batter plaster. That's right, mix to the consistency of pancake batter. Ancient secrets.

The flask is then set in a vacuum chamber. Vacuum is applied to remove voids and air pockets. Science.

The flask is then left to harden.

The spruce base is removed, leaving the wax trapped within the now hardened plaster and flask. Cooking out the wax takes several hours in the oven at extreme temperatures. The voids left in the plaster as the wax melts out are nearly an exact copy of the wax models, hopefully reflecting the carefully carved piece at the start of the process.

Lead up to the grand finale involves some math. Specific weight of metal, wax model plus .125 for the all-important button. I know, hang on.

The grand part is molten silver swirling in the crucible. The torch roars as you stir the silver magma with a carbon stick. With careful alignment of the crucible, flask and casting machine arm pull the pin to release the arm of the centrifuge contraption. The spinning force injects the molten metal into the investment flask.

Arcane spinning devices, massive heating torch blazing and molten silver spinning around, what's not to like.

It is fairly unlikely I would have pursued this art form without Christopher Cordova (Cordova Designs). We have known one another for many years now and still manage to remain friends. There is no doubt of his abilities as a master goldsmith and gem setter. His portfolio is deep and speaks for itself. His ability as a teacher, I am unable to fully express.

Chris, with his patience, calm demeanor, humor and that special art of curbing my frustration with a perfectly timed sentence was always on point with his professional advice as he continued on with his project. Thanks. Still a survivor.

Ken Alvis and son

Donna Baily

Planning for and responding to emergencies used to be my daily job but I never planned for the disaster that happened to me.

My brother's birthday celebration in August 2007 became a life changing memory for all the wrong reasons. It devastated my family and was the day I nearly lost my life.

Who would have thought a candle lighting my long skirt could do so much damage in so little time? The weeks in ICU remain a mixture of blurred memories and to this day I'm still not sure how much of it was real or if the drugs were playing tricks with my mind. However, the noises of machines, the tubes, drains, painful dressing changes and numerous surgical procedures are fixed in my mind forever.

Six years later, although I try to make the best of things most of the time, there are so many things I have lost—the use of my left hand, mobility in my legs, bend in knees, a lot of my independence, my job, my confidence, driving, ability to play music, my stamina . . . and the worst loss of all in 2010, my Dad, whom I miss dearly.

It has taken me a very long time even to get to the stage I am now and I hope I have more progress to make, but some things will never be the same and learning to 'live' and adjust with my new disabled and scarred body is a daily challenge that I continuously strive to fight.

While still on a physical and emotional roller coaster, I am beginning to realize how far I have come and how lucky I was to have a loving, caring and supportive family to help me be strong. Chatting and corresponding with other burns survivors over the last few years has been an added invaluable support in the knowledge others can truly empathize and that I am not alone.

I wish I could say I've ran a marathon, swam the channel, or climbed a mountain, but I guess I still am climbing my own personal mountain even if I lose my footing on occasion. We need to believe that there is life after burns . . . finding it is the difficult part of the journey.

In My Father's Footsteps

By Kim Dormier

This year I'm turning 47. I will be the same age my father was when he died of burn injuries from a fire at our home.

As a child, I never knew who I might find sleeping on the couch when I'd wander from my bed into the front room each morning. It might be a man sleeping off a night of drinking, a woman and her children whose home was in dire need of basic repairs, or just a hitchhiker needing a meal and a warm blanket. We lived on the Fort Hall Indian Reservation in eastern Idaho where my father ministered at the Good Shepherd Episcopal Church. We lived in the tiny parish house alongside the Church. My mother taught four year olds at the Fort Hall Reservation Head Start program; I was the youngest child, by eight years, of my three siblings.

My dad, Father Charles Allen, had a great love for the Shoshone-Bannock Indian tribe and did his best to serve them in every way he could. As the pastor of an evangelical church on the reservation, his day might include visiting a woman from the church that'd been sick, preparing for Sunday services, tending the church grounds, or picking up a confused local who needed a good meal and a place to rest during a cold winter night.

There were only a few other white kids at the grade school I attended on the reservation, but I didn't really notice. Kids are kids. The color of our skin or the kind of house we lived in was less important than just having fun. Our faith in Jesus made us all alike. Like my dad, I loved my Indian brothers and sisters, fully accepting them and they fully accepted me.

It was the week before Thanksgiving in 1974 and I was in the second grade. My mom had gone to her job at the local Head Start, I was at school and my dad was at home preparing a sermon for the Thanksgiving service the following week. That morning my mother got a call from Dad that she needed to come home right away. No other explanation but she could tell from his voice that something was terribly wrong. When she arrived home Dad was in the bedroom wrapped in their newly bought quilt. He had been very badly burned.

The fire occurred when my dad was having trouble starting a fire later that morning in the fireplace. All the wood available was wet, so he decided to use some mimeograph fluid to help get it started. A unseen spark ignited the fluid in his hands and burst onto his clothing, covering him in flames. As his clothes were in flames, he managed to climb the stairs to the bedroom and wrap himself in a quilt. Then he made the phone call to my mom.

The nearest hospital didn't have a burn unit and the Salt Lake City, Utah hospital had no room in theirs. After some phone calls were made by the doctor, they were able to find room in the burn unit at the Brooke Army Medical Center in San Antonio, Texas.

Arrangements were made for him to be life-flighted to Texas. Before he left, I was taken to the hospital to see him. That is where I got to see him in bandages loosely wrapped around his body only exposing his face and bright red fingertips caused from the burn. He wanted to give me a kiss goodbye, but the nurses wouldn't let me touch him in fear of infection. I watched as they wheeled him away and into the helicopter. I never saw him again.

My mom flew to Texas with my dad that night. A couple days later, my sister and two brothers joined her. Spending all day and night at a hospital watching my dad and other patients suffer from burns was not a place for an eight year old kid. My mom did her best to try and keep things as normal as possible for me, so she made arrangements for me to stay in Idaho with a very kind family from the Episcopal Church at a nearby city. The wife was very pregnant and she had been having complications with the pregnancy. I stayed with them for only about a week due to the arrival of the new baby.

Other arrangements had to be made for me to stay with another family.

My mom got a phone call from a woman that heard the news of my dad's accident. Sandy really wanted to help and take me in. She welcomed me into their family right away and her children accepted me too. They included me in everything

Kim Dormier as an infant with father

they did, even the daily chores, which I didn't mind doing. A little space was made for me in the corner of Kellie's room and I even had enough room for a few of my favorite toys.

I spent Christmas of 1974 with the McCoy's. That Christmas morning, I woke up to my very own, handmade Raggedy Ann and Andy dolls under the tree. Shortly after the turn of the New Year in 1975, my brothers returned to Idaho and took me into the little bedroom the McCoy family had created for me upstairs. Dave and Steve were young men with an adult responsibility. It fell upon their teenage shoulders to tell me that our dad had died. I still remember sitting on the edge of the bed and hearing the words, "Dad's in Heaven now." I don't remember much after that moment but the emotion of the day still fills my eyes with tears.

After spending six weeks in the hospital from the third degree burns over 60% of his body, Dad died on January 2, 1975. My father was buried in the church cemetery on the reservation with the people he loved and gave his life serving. I kept going to church but grudgingly. "How could a God who loved my father, a man of God, take my father away?" I demanded. It was a question that festered in my mind and heart as I grew up and grew in my resentment toward the God of my father.

I became a runner. I ran from home. I ran from my mother and my step-dad. I ran from everything and everyone I knew. I even ran from God, yet somehow ended up in a small community of Christians in Northern California. They loved and accepted me and I became keenly aware that the God I'd tried to run away from was following me. So what did I do? Rather than get comfortable or give in to His presence, I ran away again, this time to my beloved grandmother.

Life went on. I moved back to Idaho, got a job, had two beautiful children and still had this nagging awareness that the One who took my dad from me was still there, leading me, watching over me and drawing me to Himself with a love and care unlike any other.

Everywhere I ran to hide, everything I did to escape from Him, didn't work. It took nearly 35 years but He still found me. I surrendered myself to the loving embrace of my Lord and Savior Jesus. In doing so I found a long-desired purpose and meaning to my life.

This doesn't mean that the loss of my father, the pain of growing up with so many questions, or any of the other things in life have been easy. In writing this I discovered something more to God's purpose in my life. My father left this world when he was 47 years old. He gave his life loving and caring for the least of this world. He used to preach that Jesus had done the same for him.

Now I'm 47 years old and it's as if I'm taking up where he left off. I've experienced some of the worst things a child can know, but as an adult, I've discovered hope, purpose and a divine calling to share the same heavenly love my father knew, lived out and shared at every opportunity.

My story is different from most burn survivors. We each have a different survival story. If we all lived the same story, life would not only be incredibly boring, but none of us would gain anything personally. While I didn't experience the pain of fire or the physical challenges from the after effects as a burn survivor, I did live through the flames of an emotional burn. My heart, soul and mind were scarred and forever changed by losing my father. I'd never wish my own experience on anyone but I'm thankful for it. These scars have made me who I am today as I continue my path of growth as an individual: strong, courageous, intelligent, determined and so very blessed.

I think of my dad every day and wonder what it would be like to have him here with me. In a sense he is with me in my heart and mind but I have a hope and expectation of seeing him again one day in heavenly places. One day I'll see my dad again and he'll welcome me to my eternal home and lead me into the arms of my heavenly Father, safe forever.

Absorbing that from within to become a mere reflection in the mind of another like-minded.
Chago Roberto DeSantiago

Tying off at the waist being dragged day by day through that which I have not made.
Chago Roberto DeSantiago

The Real Me

By Mona Krueger

the core
my deepest heart
renewed by God
loved
whole
unscathed
protected from the stares and gawks
not devastated by cruel words
or indifference
a place of safety
my spirit alive
it defines the real me
I live from this place outward
rather than outward in
it makes all the difference

A Real Life Action Scene

By George Goodwin

I was taking the short route home. A little bit harder on the eyes but short nonetheless. The road itself wound like a snake riding down a side of lawn. I was surrounded on my left by a cove of trees and rice paddies on my right. When I say surrounded by rice paddies, I mean more

like elevated above them. It was actually a four foot (1.3 meter as they would say in Japan) drop straight into one of them, were I to make a misstep with my foot and accidentally push the accelerator instead of the brake. Fortunately I was a good driver and didn't make those kinds of mistakes.

Driving in Japan means that you are on the left side of the road driving on the right side of your car, exactly the opposite of the United States. As I crossed the stoplight flashing an eerie green in the middle of the night, I was thinking about my fiancée whose apartment I had just left and simultaneously thinking about the nice, cozy apartment that would be awaiting me at the end of my trip. I was caught off guard by the slam of my car as the passenger door was crunched beneath the hood of a car driving straight at me.

My car was a sturdy little white Honda, seventeen years old and in dire need of new tires. None of this mattered when it went over the side of the four foot drop after being hit on the passenger's side driven by a drunken Japanese driver. When it landed on its side in the paddy, my sturdy little Honda effectively trapped me in. My door was held shut by the ground and the door to my left that was struck had been partially folded, like a pancake over a fist. To complicate matters I was still wearing my seatbelt, which under normal circumstances is a good thing, protecting the driver from unnecessary wear and tear. In this case it tied me to my seat.

There was a sound of a "foom," sort of like a lover whispering in my ear something secret, something sensual—but this was not the word of a lover—only of death. Above me the gasoline in my tank had ignited, probably started by a spark that happened when my gas tank hit the edge of the road. Hardly a secret, yet secretive in a way that only someone who has undergone the experience will ever understand. I was still tied into my seat, but now in a way that would no longer assure my safety.

Adrenaline is a good thing but when in a situation where you need your wits, it can make you fumble. My fingers did, once, twice . . . on the third try I managed to unbuckle my seat belt. I knew it was only a matter of time before the whole car was engulfed in flames and the only way out was through the damaged car door. I had to push out the remains of the glass with my hands and was lucky so far as that went. Just as I was thinking myself invincible I was covered in flames, first my left side, then my right. I managed to push myself out of the vehicle before the damage got any worse.

Although I went unconscious shortly after, to a gaggle of doctors surrounding me, I was lucky to have survived the initial crash. I awoke six days later.

What is it like in a hospital? You know what it's like. I know what it's like. It's quiet. It's antiseptic. The nurses wear clean, white corners and the doctors offer you a lollipop. There are smiles. There is never laughter. Everyone is competent enough to make you feel that accidents never happen here. In short, it's what you expect in a hospital.

Let me change your expectations.

In Japan the hospitals are clean. The nurses are still wearing clean, white corners and their nursing hats that double as a sailor's hat on a ship. The doctors still wear scrubs and don white masks in order to use their scalpels on their unwitting, unconscious patients.
The similarities end there.

A burn is a burn in any language known to man. The treatment is different, however.

Before the first surgery started. Before the doctors had a chance to lower their ellipse shaped steel instruments of healing. Before the nurses had a chance to offer their assistance to the surgeons by wiping beads of sweat off their brows. Before the operation begins, the patient must be asleep. I wasn't. The anesthesiologist gave me a standard Japanese dosage of sevoflurane gas, but I was not a standard patient.

At five feet eleven inches I stood at least a head and a half taller than anyone else in the room. At 185 healthy pounds I was also at least 150 percent of their weight. As a strong swimmer I was used to a lack of oxygen and my mind was holding on to consciousness. Normally the doctor can count from 10 and the patient will lose their awareness at about seven, but I was still talking five minutes into the surgery. I wasn't talking in the semi-sane way that a drunken soul speaks because he is inebriated. I was making jokes about a Japanese cartoon (Crayon Shin-Chan) who likes to walk around on his butt nude. It was a trick that I had to do myself because I was too heavy for the doctors to lift and there were no steps to the other side of the operating table.

200 sit-ups a day, 3,000 yard daily swims and of course the exercise that the kids were giving me at school (the 500 yard prevent a finger up your rear dash) and all I could do was crack jokes about a non-existent cartoon while sliding on my gluteus maximus across a paper laden piece of leather bound plastic. So much for exercise.

Another experience of a Japanese hospital is having six year olds running around screaming and yelling to lighten up the place. Of course they come up to about your knees, so you have to be careful about stepping on them. Not that the loss would mean much—those parents would cheerfully pop another out just to spite you and yours for having squished their firstborn like a ripe tomato. I was tempted.

I was also immobile for the first three months, wrapped in a cocoon of cotton and silk. Those kids had the run of the place. I didn't get to step on even one of them.

Removing the bandages was the daily torture. Someone brilliant (doctor Yayoi?) had decided that it would be faster to remove both sets of arm bandages at the same time. What the (insert your favorite expletive here) doctor hadn't factored into account was that these burns weren't like an average sunburn—these hurt. My arms were lacking skin and took the comfort of the cotton surrounding them to be their protection from the elements within the hospital. Your skin normally protects you from blinding radiation, water, heat, cold, germs and sometimes your little sister. The cotton on my arms was serving those functions and so my arms decided to bond with it to protect themselves from the hostile environment. To make matters worse, there were at minimum three other patients who also had burns in the hospital and I was the last patient to have his cotton removed. Always.

Sometimes I could hear the thin banshee wailing of a senior crying out in pain for help and relief. At other times it was an eight-year-old girl by the name of Miho calling out for her favorite Nii-san to stop the pain. Then it was my turn to have my cotton removed.

Imagine for a second that you have no skin. Or better yet that you do have skin and you are losing it to a kitchen knife. My skin was a fragile, bloody membrane that was being pulled off centimeter by centimeter by doctors who didn't know what kind of pain they were inducing. The new skin that they had peeled from my upper thighs was thin enough that it was see-through and I could watch my sinews, cartilage and muscle working together to move my fingers while blood dripped down my arm and onto the hospital bed. I was in serious doubt that I had enough blood in my body to compensate for what I was losing. No horror film would ever scare me again because I was seeing something far worse than any film could replicate. I was seeing the inside of myself, artistically carved into the likeness of a moving machine by surgeons who had spent years honing their skills. These artisans had been given enough time to practice their art without worry of mistake or malfunction and they had sliced beneath the layers of flesh to the functioning, living part of my arm which still remained.

I screamed. I cried like a six-year-old girl who has just been kicked by a horse. My lungs were uninjured and I tried to use the sound I was forcing out of them to injure the doctors in the same way that they had hurt me. It was futile. The cotton had to be removed or it would bond permanently to my arms and no amount of expelled breath would stop the pain or the blood. I didn't shatter any windows, but not for lack of trying.

Leper Colony in Hawaii

By Alisa Christensen

My love is divided between the divine and the profane
My God is frightening, proud and quite glamorous
My lover is selfishly falling apart

Another human sacrifice to keep the world turning properly
There's beauty in anguish I'm told, just don't see it
There's celebration in poverty
Redemption in suffering
Somehow or other there's good to be made of it

My love is torn between the sublime and the scandalous
My God is petulant, spoiled and fairly abusive
My lover is selfishly falling apart

There's poetry in loneliness
Laughter in absurdity
Honor among thieves
I split my attention between hell and high water
The tropical breeze adds whimsy to solitude

My love is a razors edge delighting in unintelligible images
My God is an abstract monster gorging on fear and frailty
Sucking his sticky fingers free of blood and loss

My lover is selfishly falling apart

~I wrote this summer of 2004 while visiting my brother and nephews in Hawaii, two and a half years after the fire. They jumped into the turquoise surf with other Happy Healthy's, while I sat alone under an umbrella, nursing a broken heart. Covered in bandages and pressure garments, I felt repulsive and remembered Father Damian used to run a leper colony a couple islands over. And while I consider myself spiritual, my relationship with 'God as I see it . . . ' has always been tumultuous.

Anguish of the Human Condition

By Clare Latchem

So I sit here bewildered about what has happened and how many people in life endure this insanity. I have just had some scar revision surgery carried out to my burns and skin grafts that I have on my upper thighs. However, I would hardly classify this procedure as 'scar revision,' a term that seemed slightly equivocal to me. My body had just undergone four hours of being sliced and diced under a local anesthetic. I felt like a slab of meat in some back street butchers being prepared ready to sell, all of the off cuts being removed and placed beside me in a container.

These were the old skin grafts. They looked like strips of bacon; it was my skin, it was me! Did this really happen? My analogy of this process would be more like Buffalo Bill skinning his next victim in the classic film *Silence of the Lambs*, this was 'butchery' and I was living this nightmare.

I had sustained 18% body burns of varying degrees back in 2002. Skin grafts were applied to my thighs and my stomach, as the burns were too deep to ever heal. The burns were as a result of being caught up in a domestically abusive relationship for several years. I had suffered seven years of various abuses from physical, mental, emotional to financial. The burns were the last straw, why had I been so tenacious about this relationship? Despite the madness, I had no idea; maybe I was young and naïve?

It was a slightly normal evening in a household that usually consisted of madness. Sam and I had argued two days prior and for some reason *it hadn't* resulted in me sitting in accident and emergency for the evening with a black eye or a broken nose, this was the usual routine. We hadn't spoken for an entire two days and I had managed to keep a low profile. However I knew that this wouldn't be the end of it.

It was a Friday night and Sam's habitual drinking problem was set to escalate. His usual alcohol consumption would triple just due to the fact that it was a Friday night (a notorious excuse from an alcoholic in denial). I had tried to save him from his problem in the past but bore the brunt of that too.

I had hidden myself away from him in the bedroom that evening but it was getting late and I was hungry. I crept downstairs to make myself something to eat. Sam wasn't around so there were only one of two places he could be: one, at the pub or two, getting more alcohol. I plugged in the deep fat fryer and made myself something to eat. It was bliss sitting there enjoying my dinner without being antagonized or being made to feel inferior or worthless; however, I could feel this formidable awe that the night wasn't going to be as merciful and as calm as this.

It was getting late and I decided to get ready for bed. I came downstairs to tidy up the kitchen when the door slammed. A chill shuddered through me it was like Armageddon had arrived. I scuttled around like some frightened mouse desperately trying to clean up the mess and scamper upstairs without being noticed. But he clocked me and burst into the kitchen. He was on a mission, a mission where I never knew his objectives or motives. He began to shout in his usual slurred manner with that maleficent look he had in his eyes that spoke a million words. I was putting the fryer away at the time when he shoved me. I fell to the floor with the fryer landing on me, liters of boiling hot oil running down the front of me and onto my thighs. I don't really recall much after that as I blacked out.

The next memory I have was coming around staring at the ceiling of an ambulance, hearing its sirens and the paramedics cutting away my clothes. I could feel a state of euphoria, they had dosed me up on morphine to ease the pain and I was as high as a kite. Somehow it registered what they were doing but the severity of it was due to hit me much later on.

The burns that I had received and the treatment that was carried out were set to change my life forever. I was taken to my local hospital which was not equipped to deal with extensive burns. The nearest specialist unit was an hour away so treatment was carried out here in my hometown of Exeter, which didn't bode well for me later on in my recovery.

Now 2008, six years after the attack, the burns were a constant reminder of it, the discomfort of the burns and grafts, the vulgar appearance of the scars. I had become reclusive, depressed and I was being ostracized by society and friends were excluding me from events like swimming and going to the beach or spa. Every day, I woke up and saw my disfigurement. Every day reminded me of that night; the night my ex-partner pushed me whilst I was holding a pan of boiling hot oil. It was haunting me, I couldn't move on.

I had had little in the way of acute psychological help to support me in dealing with the trauma I had endured or assist me on living with a disfigurement. I decided to approach the plastic surgeon that had treated me initially. He suggested to me that I could have surgery to remove the grafts that I was left with; this would help reduce the significant scarring I had and ease the discomfort. Although there would be certain pre-requisites I would have to adhere to before he could carry out the surgery.

1) I had to lose a bit of weight. I had given birth to my beautiful daughter only the year before so I was carrying a bit of baby fat—I was weighing in at 65kg and his idea of an ideal weight for surgery was around the 50kg marker.

2) I had to consider if I had finished my family—what did this have to do with surgery? If I was to have more children then this would hamper the surgery he was to carry out as I had a graft across my stomach.

I was prudent about both suggestions and they were BOTH achievable. So the following two years of my life I spent obsessing over reaching my target weight, in-between trying to raise my daughter alone. I was bereft, isolated and living in solitary confinement. They were two years of hell, I ate the bare minimum and every spare minute I had without my daughter I would spend out running or at the gym (when I could afford it).

It was now 2010 and I was due to see the surgeon again. I had reached my target weight plus more, I was now weighing a mere 44kg and probably looking a little emaciated by this time, the depression had assisted with that. I couldn't function until this surgery was carried out. I went into the consulting room where I spoke with another surgeon; it wasn't the surgeon that had treated me initially. He assessed my scars and burns and then sat me down.

He proceeded to tell me that the surgery I had initially been offered was now deemed as 'low priority' on the National Health Service's list of surgical procedures. If I wanted the surgery then I would have to put my case to a funding panel; these were the people that were in charge of deciding who gets what treatment and they held the purse strings that paid for this.

I was mortified that I'd been deluded. This was a paradox, they had moved the goal posts and it was my healthcare that they were playing with. Two years were wasted adhering to criteria that were no longer bona fide. All my efforts would go unnoticed. What was I to do now? A surgical procedure that was deemed routine was now non-essential to them.

The following two years of my life were spent being passed from pillar to post seeing various counselors, psychologists and people who specialized in camouflage makeup. I took various antidepressants, I saw dermatologists—dermatologists? I had burns and skin grafts for Christ's sake not a skin condition. Even the dermatologist was as confounded as I was about my arrival into his consulting room! I was given creams and lotions all of which seemed nonsensical and counterproductive, and at what cost to these people?

Surely the surgery didn't amount to anything like what they were paying to fob me off. Any which way the NHS could avert giving me funding for surgery; I didn't understand the logic of any of it. I collated all of this evidence and forwarded it to the funding panel (or the Gestapo as I later named them); this was becoming a bureaucratic nightmare. My file was continuing to grow and in my mind the evidence I presented suggested that I was a likely candidate for surgery but my case was continually rejected.

I decided to see various private plastic surgeons to get some advice. I wasn't really in a position to do anything about it; I was a single mum living off a nominal amount of money. Nevertheless, I cut corners on my living expenses so that I could put money aside to pay for a private consultation. I'm not sure what I hoped to achieve from this but maybe they could help me present my case to the NHS. Which they did. A combination of letters were sent to the panel stressing the reasons for my surgery and how I would be likely to gain some form of benefit from it– all declined.

The panel said that my pursuit for surgery was purely cosmetic and that after surgery I would still be left with scars anyway. So it was unlikely that surgery would have any benefit to me and my quality of life. I approached my local Member of Parliament for help, to which he made enquiries to the Royal College of Surgeons based in London. They were responsible for maintaining and enhancing professional standards in surgery; he enquired why somebody with significant burns that were affecting them could not access treatment. They were mystified too, another letter to add to my compendium of evidence already submitted.

My case was presented a final time to the funding panel in 2012 to which it was then forwarded directly to an 'appeals panel.' Holy crap, how many people are being employed here just to review a surgical procedure that should have been routine? This is an example of nonsensical processes and wasted taxpayers' money, policy makers on fat salaries making unethical decisions affecting tax paying citizens. This was getting far too political and as much as I am a benevolent person, I can't save this country from its failing health system. I have to remain egocentric about this, this is about MY surgery.

I was informed that I needed to personally present my case to the appeals panel (I hadn't been allowed this privilege prior to this point). Policies also stated that I wasn't allowed a lawyer present at the hearing either. What kind of communist dogma was this? However they would kindly provide me with an advocate who knew nothing of my case until the week before the hearing . . . hmm this all seemed slightly biased and insensitive to me. I remained pessimistic about this decision-making process. The likelihood of me being given any kind of funding for my surgery seemed remote.

On October 23, 2012 I attended the panel meeting and the outcome was reached on October 29th. I had been awarded funding! The decision reached was that I had demonstrated that surgery was more than cosmetic and that my burns and grafts were causing me discomfort and affecting my psychological well-being and quality of life.

On December 5th, I had my first dose of surgery from which I am still recovering, and it will be a while before I can reap the benefits from it. I guess that's the malevolent nature of burn scars and the arduous task of the healing process mentally, emotionally and physically.

Yolonda Hawkins

I was burned in a cooking accident at age three in Pacific Grove, California. My mother was cooking and I wasn't even in the house. She heard a noise upstairs and knew it had to be my little sister who was a year old and must have crawled up the stairs. She went to get her and became distracted from her cooking. By the time she came back down, there was smoke billowing from the kitchen and the pan she was making tacos in was on fire with grease spattering. She was going to throw it out the window but remembered there was dry grass and worried it would catch fire. She decided to bring the pan through the living room and opened the front door as my little friend Tracy and I were coming in. She yelled and told us to run out of the way, which we did, but a gust of wind came up and the nylon turtleneck I was wearing caught fire and melted onto my skin. My mother, who was twenty-two at the time, tried to take my clothes off, which unfortunately took the melted material and my skin with it.

Luckily, two nurses that lived across from us saw the whole thing. One called the hospital and told them we were on our way. Monterey Community was a few miles away and the other nurse rushed my mom and I to the hospital. I had many surgeries through the years as I was burned on my face, neck, chest, right shoulder, arm and back. It was a hard road to recovery and I grew up being teased and stared at and got into many fights. As the years went by I was treated just like my sister doing chores, learning to cook and clean, play, getting spanked and having a very normal life. My parents didn't allow me to not do things on my own and wouldn't allow me to say I can't.

I would, however, try to hide some of my scars with long sleeves and turtlenecks, even in 100 degree Los Angeles weather. One day, I decided I wasn't going to do it anymore as a teenager.

I put on a short-sleeved regular shirt and got ready to go out the door. My mom said, "Don't you wanna wear this instead Yoller?"

I said, "No, I don't care who stares anymore they are gonna do it anyway." I believe that was when I gained some independence.

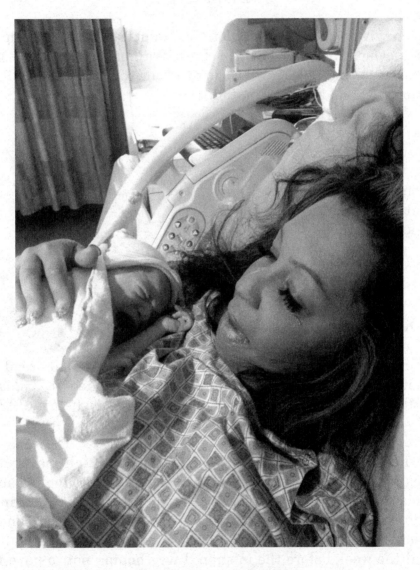

Yolonda Hawkins and son, Adian

Excerpt from *Singed Miracles*

By Laura Brixey

We were given many pamphlets of information regarding our situation. One was on PTSD, or Post Traumatic Stress Disorder. Much to our surprise, Richard wasn't the one to be affected by PTSD; it was me who had all the symptoms.

I was not really even aware of post traumatic stress, much less the symptoms. It is difficult to deal with something if you don't know about it, or even if you are affected by it. Richard had been alerted to it to check the symptoms for himself. He read the pamphlet, then looked online and learned more information. He then strongly urged me to read the information he had found. I subconsciously avoided it, being too exhausted, unable to concentrate and too overwhelmed. Which actually were some of the symptoms.

It was I from the beginning, with the flashback nightmares again and again that would startle me awake night after night causing insomnia. After about a week or more without sleep in the beginning of our journey, I finally called my doctor and got a prescription for a mild sleeping medication. Since I had just seen her for my annual physical the week before the mishap, I was hoping not to have to go in to see her again in person. I called her office and left a message something like this: "Hi Dr. Smith. We've had a situation at my house and I'm not sleeping. I was hoping you would be able to give me a mild prescription to help. Since I was just in to see you and considering your tight schedule as well as mine, I was hoping to not have to come in. Is that possible?"

Bless her heart! She called it in for me so all I had to do was to go get it. She probably got a clue as to my situation when she called and was greeted with the "burn unit" salutation. It was wonderful to be able to sleep again and get recharged! But I didn't want to become dependent on sleeping aids so that was only a short-term fix.

I, also, had a difficult time relaxing my muscles. They were constantly tense, it seemed. I didn't even realize it most of the time until my muscles would start to almost cramp. I would tell myself to relax, concentrating on individual muscle groups and after a few minutes, my muscles would actually begin to relax. But since I also had a difficult time concentrating, I would soon be thinking about everything else and before I realized it, all my muscles would be tense again. And I would repeat the process again. In retrospect, I should have gone for help in dealing with PTSD. I would have recovered much more quickly if I had known what I was dealing with. As it was, it took me a couple of years to recover.

Which leads into another of our journeys: it was about mid-February when Richard began to limp. He tried to do his home therapy on his left ankle, but it was so very sore that he just couldn't. His ankle was so swollen I couldn't get his compression sock on that foot at all. When we went to therapy that morning, the therapist took one look at it and canceled the session.

We had an appointment to see the doctor that same morning. When Dr. K. began his debridement routine, he took a biopsy specimen from the ankle and sent it off for analysis. Dr. K suspected that Richard had contracted the dangerous antibiotic resistant staph infection, called MRSA. The doctor sent us over to another part of the hospital campus to be fitted for a removable walking cast boot to keep his ankle stabilized. The doctor also set an appointment for us to go to an infection specialist as soon as possible.

It turned out to be a really long day and it wasn't over yet. There was more to come. In retrospect, it was about the worst day of our whole ordeal after the very first week. We were so tired and so naïve about some things, we nearly fell into a trap. We had started our day at 5:00 that morning and left the house about 7:30. By the time we finished seeing the doctor and getting the cast, we didn't get home until about 2:00. Exhausted doesn't begin to describe how tired we were, emotionally and physically drained. And hungry too. We were really looking forward to some quiet time to rest, to do nothing and see no one. Richard had gone to the back room when the doorbell rang. I opened the door to find a scruffy, unkempt young man standing there. Apparently, he'd started attending our church a short time before and found out about Richard.

"Is this the house of the guy who got hurt?" he inquired.

"Who are you?" I asked.

"Is this where the man lives who got hurt?" he repeated himself. "I came to help."

About that time Richard came out from the bathroom and said, "Hi Billy." (Not his real name).

"Oh, it is," Billy said, and with that, he turned and waved his ride away. From behind him, I was waving, trying to stop his ride from leaving! But the car continued down the street while Billy made his way into our home, stepping around me.

"OK, you can stay a half of an hour," I sighed. "I need to go get some new medicine and you can keep Richard company while I'm gone." With that, I got Richard settled in the recliner and Billy into the rocker close by with a glass of lemonade.

It took nearly an hour to get the prescription filled and to return home. I immediately checked in to see how Richard was doing. Right away, I could see that Billy had re-arranged some of the furniture to make himself at home. He said something about seeing Richard's shoes and things. "Aha! You've been caught! You weren't supposed to get up," I teased, shaking my finger at Richard.

"No, no, no, he didn't get up, I went and looked myself," Billy lied. Even though he was defending Richard, it sent up big red flags. Richard was not impressed but he said nothing. Instead, he asked if I could get Billy something to eat. "Sure," I said, "We have some leftover Chinese food from last night. I could warm some of that." Billy wrinkled his nose and shook his head. Hmmmm!

Before I had a chance to respond, Richard suggested, "We have a little of that chicken and potato dish left. How about some of that?" Billy smiled, nodding his head enthusiastically.

Billy and Richard followed me into the kitchen and I began digging through the fridge. Richard flopped down on the sofa in the den not far away and soon began snoring loudly. While I prepared his food, Billy chatted non-stop, telling me about all of his ailments and the drugs he was taking. My ears burned! Big red flags all over the place!

I placed his plate of food on the table and watched him settle in and eat. I could tell in the pit of my stomach he was planning on staying for more than just the afternoon. I can't really explain it, I just knew. I had to be alone, I had to get help. So I excused myself, went back to my bedroom and lay on my bed. Every muscle in my body was sort of throbbing and vibrating. I just ached all over.

"Lord," I began. "I don't want to be selfish or mean but I just don't have any more energy to take care of anybody else. How do I handle this situation? What do I do?" Then I was quiet for about two minutes when I got my answer. I can't describe it, it just came into my heart and I knew what to do. I got up and went back into the kitchen.

"Want a piece of pie?" I asked Billy.

"Oh, YES!" he smiled as I served him a nice slice. When he was about done with it, I offered another piece and he happily accepted. Then I wrapped up two more pieces of pie for him and said, "You can take this home with you for later."

The expression on his face told it all. He looked at me so bewildered. I then asked if he lived close enough to walk or did he need to take a bus? He said he didn't live that far but had a bad knee and the bus didn't go that way.

"Well, then, I'll take you." I said.

"I need to go have a smoke and think about it." Aha! New revelation, he smokes too.

"No, there's nothing to think about. You can smoke at home," I said. It took me about fifteen minutes to get him away from the table and into the car. Then it took another five minutes to get him out of my car at his house. He begged to come back to help in any way I needed, yard work, housework, anything. I thanked him and let him know to call first before coming over. But I wasn't about to open the door to him again.

When I got back home, Richard confirmed my feeling about Billy and filled me in on what had transpired while I was gone. Not only had Richard shown Billy the shoes and such, but three times he asked to be fed. We both had the idea he was looking for someone new to take care of him. We saw Billy at church once or twice after that before he moved on.

About two or three weeks later, Billy's estranged wife called asking for him. I said that he wasn't here; she acted as if she didn't believe me. She said Billy had given her this number and said he'd be here for a long time. Our suspicions were confirmed. I've since learned that it is not uncommon to have people come around who know you have drugs in the house for the sick. In our distraction, naivety and exhaustion, we nearly fell into this trap. Again, we thanked God for protecting us. That could have been a real mess.

Battle Scars

By Trevor Beam

I was burned in December 2001 when I was thirteen. I was out at my Dad's house; his girlfriend gave me a lighter and told me to go burn some garbage. There was a lot of garbage in a small can. My friend and I lit some paper but it only smoked. We decided to get some gas because I thought it would burn faster but it didn't, it blew up in my face and I caught on fire. I ran into the house on fire. They had no water running at the moment; my father's girlfriend told me to go back outside and she threw rocks from the gravel driveway on me because she didn't know what else to do. I pulled my clothes off and walked into the tub. I think it was cold.

The ambulance took me up the road to a big field. The helicopter was waiting. They put me on a gurney took me to Legacy Emanuel. Sponge on a stick dipped in water to wet my mouth. They scrubbed my skin to get the dead skin off. I met Doctor Polito, what a wonderful man he is. When I was in the Burn Unit, I met this guy who fell asleep with a cigarette in his mouth. They had a school inside the hospital because I was getting to miss school at Cascade. I went to physical therapy every day to learn to do everything all over again, like walking or getting in the bathtub. I liked the hospital beds because they had hydraulics where you could go up and down. This was better than going to school.

It's hard to talk, to get my frustrations out sometimes. It seems like the doctors in the hospital weren't that helpful. It was traumatic what I went through. The first doctor that I went to wouldn't give me my medical history that I needed for another doctor I was seeing. I don't know if that's illegal that they wouldn't give me my medical history but I went in raising hell. I said, "I will pay you whatever it costs to copy the whole file!"

And he still wouldn't give it to me. I needed it for social security; I think it was for benefits. To this day he still refuses to give them to me.

When I went back to school I was in the ninth grade and I got bullied. I would ignore it and tell them, "these are my battle scars." Once I got onto the football team in high school they didn't really make fun of me. My coach understood. After I got burned, I went to Texas to visit my mom's family. I was walking down the street  alone, wearing shorts and some strangers ran over to me and said, "oh my God what happened to you?!" I told them I was burned. I didn't go into detail but just said, "these are my battle scars."

Sometimes when I start talking about it I start shaking really bad, like a leaf. But I am lucky to be alive. It has been really hard to talk about it because my dad's an asshole and he doesn't listen to me. I can't talk to him about it. He doesn't take any responsibility.

My stepdad had always been a sounding board, someone I could talk to. If I was having a hard time or any troubles he was always there to help me figure it out. He died when I was nineteen.

My mom has a rental house and as he was cleaning up he didn't mix the ammonia right and the windows were shut so there was no ventilation. He felt really sick afterwards and went to the doctor who told him to come back the next day. But the next morning my stepfather was already gone. It was such a shock to my mom and I; we miss him so much. My mom tries to help me as much as she can.

I haven't been able to write about my burn accident until a writing workshop in the burn unit, run by Write Around Portland in 2009. I still have anxiety (PTSD) from the injury over a decade ago.

'Shooter' by Alisa Christensen

I was confined within four walls of a dark sterile room. The society we lived in, in Bangladesh, was not welcoming of anyone scarred.

Labonya Siddique

'Imperfect' individuals were ostracized with no hope for love,
marriage, career or acceptance.

Labonya Siddique

AN ARCHITECT'S HOME

By Sara Mcliroy

Our heart like a home
Can become burdened, battered and worn
But one can rebuild and strengthen
Begin with a well-built foundation and solid structure
Choose timber that endures
And frame with integrity
Erect walls of character
And insulate to encircle hope and faith
Build doors with principle
And create rooms for inspiration
Be generous and lavish with windows and skylights
Compose a fireplace made of stone
With embers burning brightly as the center of your home
For if your home is open and inviting
There will always be joy and laughter
Surround your home with love
And you will never be alone
Your home and heart are as one

Our Secret

By AnnMarie Balik

The year was 1969 and I was a seven-year-old exploratory child. I was staying at my aunt's house for a week or so. On the day of the burn injury, I was playing with paper cut-out dolls in the living room of her home. In the afternoon, my aunt, who volunteered at the local Catholic Church, informed me that it was time to go over to the church to perform various duties over there.

I had been with my two older sisters (in the church) on an occasion in the past when I had watched them re-light votive candles that had only a little bit of wick remaining. Once the last bit of wick was burned down, then they inserted new candles into the votive containers. On this day my sisters were not with me. I asked my aunt the same question that I had heard my sisters ask. "Ann, Can I burn down the candles?"

She said, "Yes, but don't get burned."

I was unable to reach the candles, which were on a tiered rack behind the altar, so I climbed on top of the altar and was in a squatting position which allowed me access to the long wooden stick to light the candles with. As I began to light the votive candles, it didn't take very long for the lace on my dress to ignite from the heat of the candles and my dress began to burn as well as the skin beneath the dress. I attempted to snuff out the fire with my hands but was not successful.

My legs locked up from fear, shock and trauma. Once I was able to move again, I got down from the altar and sought out my aunt. I walked through the pulpit area of the church and into an adjoining room where she was mending a priests' vestment. I stood in the

doorway and called out to her. When she saw me ablaze in the doorway, she ran to me and put the flames out with her hands. She lifted the burned dress off and wrapped a sheet around me.

We returned to the pulpit area where she continued with church chores of wiping the communion wafer tray and wine glass and swept the floor where I stood while waiting for her to finish the chores. Next, we walked to her home, which was across the alley. My uncle was working in the garden and saw us as we approached. He looked at the burn and commented, "Gee, I've burned my finger but nothing ever like that before." We went into the house so my aunt could make two phone calls. One was to a neighbor to ask her to sweep in the church by the votive candle rack. The other call was to the local doctor, who had to be called into the office on a non-workday. The doctor gave me a booster shot and said I had to go to Children's Hospital in St. Paul, MN, about two hours away.

With all the delays, it was approximately three to four hours after the burn incident that I finally arrived at the hospital. A doctor was standing in the doorway, waiting for me to arrive. I was in shock but somehow alert enough to walk into the building. The doctor looked at the burn and stated, "You're still burning. We have to put silver oxide on you." That is the last I remember for quite some time.

When I awoke, the doctor was present and said that he could tell that I tried to put the fire out because both of my hands had first degree burns with blisters on them. He also told me that I was lucky because the fire had come very close to reaching my hair.

I recall having my blood taken three times a day to check the blood gases. Intravenous (I.V.) lines with blood transfusions and fluids flowed into me constantly. I was told not to move my legs or feet as that could pull the I.V. needles out of my feet and it would be more pain to re-insert the I.V. needles. As an aid to have me not move my feet, they were tied to the bed. There I lay for a month with only being able to move my head and left arm and to raise my pelvis onto and off of the bedpan. One statement I heard frequently was: "Turn your head to the left to vomit so you don't ruin the sterile dressings on your right side." My trunk and right arm were mummy wrapped with gauze and elastic wrappings over that. My lower body was bare-naked with genitals totally exposed to anyone who came into the room. There was an apparatus over my abdomen and thighs, which was in the shape of a half circle. This device had some type of light in it that was to help with healing of the area where skin had been removed for grafts. I felt extremely vulnerable and devastated while I lay there with my privates exposed.

Besides the initial event of being burned and awaiting treatment, the other most painful incident was when a doctor came into the room with three or four others. He said he was going to remove the gauze wrap from my thighs and abdomen. I asked if it was going to hurt. He replied, "It will be like a bee sting." It turned out to be an episode that I recall as being tortured. The others that were present held my little body down while I screamed, agonized and writhed in intense pain while the doctor ripped the gauze off from where the skin had been removed for grafting purposes. Every time that I raised my trunk and fought with all my strength to get away from them, I was pushed back down. Finally, the pain had reached an unbearable level that I could no longer tolerate physically, mentally, emotionally, nor psychologically and I had a near death experience. This was the biggest fight of my life and became the darkest night of the soul.

The bulk of my time and energy in the hospital was spent sleeping, as I did not have the energy or the life force to remain awake. I was barely able to keep my eyes open at meal times. All of my bodily energies were focused on healing and staying alive.

My aunt came to visit me one time and said, "You don't have to tell anyone. This will be our secret."

The day before I was going to be released from the hospital, the doctor told me I was going to walk down the hallway with him. Somehow I was put into a standing position while the doctor put his arm around my waist. I attempted to walk but all of my muscles felt like jello. I had absolutely no muscle control nor ability to ambulate down the hall after having been bed-ridden for a month. The walking experience was more like he pushed and pulled me alongside of him.

The accident happened towards the end of summer vacation. I was told that school was delayed one week to accommodate my release date from the hospital. I returned to school on the first day of third grade with my Mom walking me into the classroom. I recall sitting at my desk and crying, as it was very difficult to be present at school. And, my body was still in a great deal of pain. While outside on the playground during recess, schoolmates attempted to lift up my school dress uniform to see the burn scars.

When I was in the sixth grade, I went home for lunch periods and collected the mail. When I saw appointment reminder cards appear in the mail for upcoming doctor appointments, I would tear them up and throw them away as I was very reticent towards any further burn evaluation and/or treatment due to the degree of pain and trauma previously experienced. I recall that a doctor had said that I could have re-constructive surgery on my breast but I was never able to return to the doctor.

I received third degree burns on the right side of my torso, from the clavicle down to the navel. The area included the breast, underarm and part of the biceps and triceps area. Skin was removed from my thighs and abdomen for grafting purposes.

When I was a bit older, one of my sisters informed me that she had overheard the doctor tell our dad that if it had happened to her that she would not have survived. Even though she was two years older than me, she was always an inch shorter and about ten pounds lighter and we weren't over sized kids. I realize now that I was in critical condition with a serious injury.

When I was in my late twenties, I visited the church where the incident occurred and also the hospital medical records department to read my chart. The medical records employee inquired why I wanted to look at the micro-fiche chart. I replied, "It's a part of my life that I don't know about." From the chart, I learned that I had been sick (vomiting frequently due to a side effect of ether that was utilized as anesthesia at that time). I also learned that my right nipple was removed and a biopsy was performed on it. The report stated that the nipple was " . . . black and leathery."

I am now 52 years old. I have had a tremendous amount of energy work during the healing journey over the course of my life. It has only been the last two years that I am no longer functioning from a stance of shock trauma and flight or fight mode.

An experience that was to be kept a secret has now come out of the shadows and I am grateful for that.

P.S.

What was the necessity of performing a biopsy on the nipple when it was clearly " . . . black and leathery" from a third degree burn?

Why the doctor didn't remove the gauze wrap from the grafting sites in a less torturous manner is beyond comprehension.

Why my aunt delayed treatment for me is unbelievable.

What are the long-term side effects of ether on a seven year old?

The injury and circumstances in this anthology do not define me. I am so much more.

AnnMarie's watercolor painting

In Fragments Lays the Truth Which if Found May Not be Unbelievable

By Chago Robert DeSantiago

They will forget if they are not always able to see the reminders, or the devastation of what had occurred, and they will never fully be able to understand no matter how much they say that they love you. This is about a child that would have every thing taken from them whether intentionally or not. A new birth so to speak. There are times when I think that this child was born and was given too much, so some of it had to be taken back. It has been like this my whole life and even to this day it is like this during the hard times, the dark times. I will refer to myself as the child, because I am still a child in so many ways. It seems like there is so much missing from that child that there can be no other explanation for much of what I go through; I am childlike even still as a man.

There is a side to recovery that seems to last a lifetime; it is that moment when you think that you have overcome the most difficult of obstacles only to find that you have a whole new set of them laying ahead of you. It is almost as if the entire world is against you feeling any better so that you can finally be yourself. If I am to tell a tale of what I have gone through it will not be pretty, if I am to write it in a certain way, it will not come out right at all. So here we go, I can only imagine what it is like to have my flesh being melted in an exothermic reaction of saliva and acid inches below my infant-sized brain. It is not very pretty, but I try to imagine it so often that it is no longer uncomfortable for me. It is common and nothing out of the ordinary, no one will ever know what it was like to writhe around in anguishing pain, screaming in agony until I could no longer make any sounds at all as my mouth melted. There was probably a little foaming at the mouth too but I do not remember any of it.

I blame myself. I am the one that got into that acid, I'm the one that poured it into my mouth; for me, there was no playing with matches, no smoke, there was no fire all. I had what I assume to be instant burning flesh teeth and bone.

I was fifteen months old. Something that I had done in my fifteen months of life so far was so bad that I deserved to burn myself with acid. It was all my fault and I am sorry for what ever it is that I have done. You can not change my mind, believe me I am still trying.

I am sitting on the floor of a hospital waiting room, I've been here for hours and hours. Lucky for me I got here early, well not too early, I have two dates for valentines day which happens to be today; one with an audiologist and the other with an ear, nose and throat specialist. What I can still do is describe the bathroom in the home where my accident happened in enough detail to make my mother cry. The bathroom is still in my dreams in an almost haunting kind of way, so is the house, which is still standing although it has undergone some cosmetic changes, much like I have since that day.

Well, I seem to have perfect hearing with the exception of having central tinnitis now, which is a certain type of tinnitis that is between the ears and is vertical. This pinpoints it right in the center of my brain, which really fucks with my ability to put things in order, focus, or concentrate. I wish I could use it as an excuse to quit listening but I am not able to allow myself that freedom. I think I still care too much; there is a side of life that I have only known for fifteen months of my 39-year-old life. As there is no way to get back to that side of life, I am only able to live this life the best I can as a survivor of chemical burns sustained in my infancy. I find myself in a constant struggle with reality and what I perceive to be as real; I find that I have no real basis for any kind of reality, yet I am always forced to face the realities of life so most times I act inappropriately. I expect what I feel is what most others would feel in the same situations but I am sadly mistaken most times. The lessons learned are very hurtful and many times they are repeated. As if I am stuck on repeat or I expect every one I meet to be in sync with my wants, my needs, my desires, hopes and dreams but they never are. I find myself alone and seeking isolation from any and all who may try to console me.

Driving aside my self-parted road to fading glory

There was that one time I knew that I would always be different. There was that one time I knew I was not the same. There was that one time I knew I would have to struggle my whole life. There was this thing that happened that could not have ever happened to anyone else. There are things that have happened that I cannot imagine happening to anybody else. There are those times when I do not even feel like a body at all, I feel like pain and that is all. There are times when my dreams seem like my only life, and then when I awake my life seems as if it is the dream, and then I awaken or sleep, I am never quite sure. There is this feeling that I need an answer that no longer exists. There are times when I feel the greatest love that can ever be known. There have been times when I have died, I was brought back and often I wonder why. There are always thoughts racing around in my mind. Sometimes I wonder if all that I am is racing thoughts. There are times when I have built the biggest walls to keep the world out. There are times when I have been behind walls for too long. There are times when I cannot feel and it feels like nothing. There are times when not feeling has been my only defense. There are times when I must accept all of this. There are the most times when I just keep ignoring this. All in all, I have been the greatest I have ever been while being the very least that I can be.

The only way that I have made it this far is by hoping. I have faith that there will always be a better tomorrow. So I prepare for that tomorrow by being the best person that I am able to be this day. It is not always easy to do, I encounter heavy opposition and the road is littered with distractions and obstacles, some of which are of my own design. I do believe in a God, a Creator, a Spiritual entity; I am just not sure how to believe, so I have my own way I pray when I go to bed. I pray when I wake up, I Pray before and after a meal and I do it because it makes me feel good for what I am lucky enough to have. Every day that I get myself to live even the tiniest bit is a breakthrough for me. There has been lots of help too, even though I am the most stubborn of people when it comes to asking for help.

I have always been blessed with someone willing to help me. My family has and will always be there for me, as I try to be for them. My friends and my loved ones, without whom I would have been the loneliest that I could have ever imagined being. This has been a small telling of my life as a Chemical Burns Survivor. No two Burns Survivors are the same; we all go through different things. The only things we have in common are the echoes of what once was which haunt our daily lives. If this excerpt from my life has been a bit hard to follow, well please excuse me for that because sometimes it is much harder to live, and it has been this way my whole life.

Life capturing the living we were both smiling knowing the beauty that would be shared.
Chago Roberto DeSantiago

Beautifying that which will lead to our ultimate destruction is not only art but is life
a tree will only ever be a beautiful tree.
Chago Roberto DeSantiago

Clamoring

By Mona Krueger

voices in the wind
clamoring for attention
seeking resolution
some profound meaning

wasted suffering would be the real tragedy
like the dark side calling me
to wallow in self-pity and hopelessness
a black hole with no appeal
death

let the wind carry me out
resolute
I want to dwell in sunlight
have triumph in my life
some good realized

a sacred sabbath
rising above circumstances
at peace with who I am . . .

Excerpt from *Facing The Truth*

By Bethany Storro

I tried to hide my wounds and would make up excuses for my injured body when someone noticed. But once in a while I would confess to my husband that I had had a bad day and deliberately inflicted damage. A couple of times I even admitted that seeing a kitchen knife made me want to really hurt myself. Appalled and concerned, he urged me to get help.

I saw a therapist for a while, but she didn't have a diagnosis for me beyond OCD and her only advice was for me to wear gloves full-time so I couldn't touch my face. I went on a psych medication and it did help a bit with the OCD and the length of time in the bathroom, but not enough in my estimation. Like a lot of people on medications for psychological issues, once a person feels a little bit better, he or she can wrongly conclude they are no longer necessary, when just the opposite is true.

Taylor tried to help me manage the obsessions. We covered the bathroom mirror so I couldn't spend hours in front of it but of course I would just uncover it. For the next attempt, he took down the mirror and hid it offsite where I couldn't find it. After two days I became desperate without my fix and rummaged through old boxes in the garage until I found a little half-broken one. In the end we decided that ridding our lives of mirrors just wasn't practical for either of us, or any real solution to my problems.

Not having an accurate diagnosis, coupled with not being given the right medication, caused me to experience little improvement over the next year. Still hating myself, I figured there wasn't any more help to be found. I stopped taking the meds and believed it was up to me to keep trying to fix my problems on my own, without those seemingly useless therapeutic tools.

And not knowing any better, I clung to that belief.

My story with Taylor kept unfolding as I shared deeper things with my counselor.

My unhappiness grew and grew with him, with all my issues and with my life. I never questioned his love, but I wondered what it would be like to live on my own and enjoy a measure of freedom I had never experienced being married at such a young age. I felt trapped by circumstances, not the least of which was my own dysfunction. Some other life called to me, one that would fill this gaping hole of depression and dreadful feelings that I experienced every day.

I was tired of fighting the image in the mirror, hiding my struggles and trying to be a good wife when I knew my inadequacies on too many levels. Just like having those new clothes but never feeling good enough about myself to wear them, I had this deep sense that I wasn't good enough for Taylor and never would be.

A typical weekend for us could never just be about living life together or doing anything spontaneous without my OCD and BDD interfering.

Not ever.

We would get up Saturday morning, and knowing how long it would take for me to get ready, Taylor would grab me a coffee and then go to work for several hours. I would text him when I was ready to officially start the day. Once we met up again later in the afternoon, we would walk our dog, run errands and usually have a nice dinner out somewhere.

How I spent those early hours is part of the life I hid for the seven years of our marriage. When we eventually moved into our own home about year number three, my obsessive tendencies kicked up a notch.

On average it took me four hours to clean our small apartment every day. I started in the bedroom making the bed, picking up, dusting and vacuuming. Then I would tackle the bathroom and clean the toilet, shower, sink, floor and mirror, making them spotless. On to the living room I went with the same routine and then to the kitchen.

Once the basic cleaning was done, I went back into each room and tackled drawers, closets, baskets and bins. To get sidetracked by a wayward thought or lose focus compelled me to start a task all over again. Every detail had to be just so. Once I finished the cleaning and straightening, I then headed to the mirror to work on my appearance, taking up more chunks of time obsessing over this and that.

Every day.

Heaven help me if I had an 8:00 a.m. appointment somewhere. That meant my day started at 5:00 a.m. or earlier to get it all done.

Twice a week I cleaned out the fridge. For most people that would mean purging anything with green growth on it. For me it meant removing all items and washing down each shelf and crevice. I washed a load of cleaning rags every day and used copious bottles of dish soap.

My husband and I often ate dinner out to avoid the time I would have to spend cleaning after preparing the meal. Some days it was just easier to ignore my behavior and find ways around it, both of us trying to cope and maintain some semblance of a normal life together.

At other times we would sit down and make a list of the absolute essential things for me to do, with the goal of cutting out the obsessive ones. It gave me permission to reduce and manage my OCD but the results were always temporary. This cyclical pattern of making a plan, failing to follow it, crying out to Taylor and making a new plan only perpetuated itself.

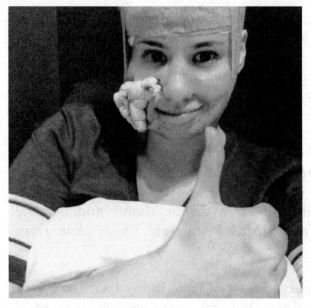

The reality was that in the end I sabotaged my marriage, being helpless to change my thinking and actions. The need to escape seemed logical at the time. My unhappiness and frustration with myself made me want to change my life in some drastic way but I didn't know which direction help lay in.

Taylor could see me slowly drifting away emotionally, apathetic and so unhappy. He would look at me with the pain of the world in his eyes. I hated hurting him and it only added to my sense of guilt, the need to punish myself and somehow escape my life. We talked about getting some counseling together but never acted upon the thought. That was the start of our relationship splintering.

The day I asked for a divorce will stay in my mind forever. We had been married for seven years. He cried when I told him what I wanted and simply asked, *"Why?"* His loyalty through so much staggered me. I had no answer just a wrenching certainty that I had to get out, that I was not enough, pushing him away in the process.

Taylor wanted to give me more time to make sure of my decision so we made up a separation plan that would leave the door open in case I changed my mind. He had lined up a job in another city for a six-month stint. I could have gone with him and lived in a hotel but instead the plan became that I would stay with some family members in Idaho. It would give me time to really think things through.

That time away from each other only confirmed my warped plan. That cocktail of BDD, depression and OCD was ruling my life and destroying all sound reasoning.

Neither one of us had told anyone of our separation but the family began to guess, seeing our odd behavior and living arrangements.

Divorcing him made me happy for about two seconds. The regrets rolled in almost immediately. My life and issues took a dreadful turn for the worse.

Within a couple of months I was actively trying to get him back, texting him often. My pleading would be something like: *"I'm so sorry. I made a big mistake. Can we work something out?"* He would write back different thoughts but all with one theme and not the answer I wanted to hear: *"I don't think I can do it. I need time. I am really hurt."*

But those words actually preserved a bit of hope in my heart so I kept texting, almost begging at times but my desperation must have appeared extremely unhealthy.

And it was.

I knew he felt bitter that I had walked away, and with time, he probably also realized what a dysfunctional life we had been living and was wary of stepping back into that old regime. Nothing had changed about me. I couldn't blame him.

So I had to let him go.

Back at the mental health facility my counselor talked me through the regret and heartache. I certainly hadn't gotten over him or worked through the grief, let alone my depression. It had been a major trigger for my suicide attempt. Through counseling I let myself begin to feel the pain of that loss and it caused me to make some additional plans but not of the constructive variety.

After two months at the facility my suicidal tendencies had quieted. The staff safely let me have a razor to shave my legs at this point and other self-care tools that I might have used for another attempt earlier. But my desire for self-punishment and the need to have my feelings jumpstarted hadn't quite gone away. That craving for pain had been steadily creeping back up on me.

It is not so much that it will ever be too little lack of wanting through no lack of trying.
Chago Roberto DeSantiago

As if the day went and as if the day was and as if the day never.
Chago Roberto DeSantiago

Paul Peterson

I don't know the make and model of the baby, but if it's anything like my daughter, he or she is going to be a delight. April was the easiest baby. It's still hard to believe I'm going to be a Granddad at fifty-one.

December '04 was the house fire. I'd gotten intoxicated and was sleeping; I think this individual, who I had a restraining order against, had something to do with the fire; but the fire department and the police got no information from me, I was in a medically induced coma for four and a half months. Since there was no sign of a break in, they concluded it was 'accidental,' caused by a lit cigarette. But I smoked 'Tops' roll your own. That tobacco goes out if you set it down (No saltpeter). Doesn't compute.

If I had somebody that wasn't a temp, or someone advocating for me, things might have been different. I was low on the totem pole for a fire investigation. That's caused contention for ten years. Was I so drunk that I did this to myself, or because I was inebriated, she got me? She had told me, "I'm going to kill you," and I believed her. Either way, I haven't come to terms with it.

When I did come to it was in a nursing home; finding out I had been disfigured was a trip: 30% total burn, head, neck, shoulders and hands, 3rd and 4th degree. I lost my nose, eyelids, ears and the use of my fingers. Still, the fire itself was minor, the disfigurement was uncomfortable but I could live with it. Nothing compares to the CVA or 'Cerebral Vascular Accident' I had while sedated. The medication prescribed while I was in a coma had a side effect of stroke.

It affected my right side motor skills, stability and gave me short-term memory loss. It caused aphasia (loss of ability to understand or express speech, caused by brain damage) and stuttering. Being burned affected my looks and that's hard for some people to take; but the CVA makes me sound slow, stupid and makes me stumble and fumble for words. That's the worst, because I'm fairly smart, well read and have a big vocabulary, I just can't access it.

In '07 I was moved to The MacDougal's House; I'm a recovering alcoholic and drug addict but I wasn't getting my drugs from homeboy on the corner, the system was furnishing my addiction to opiates. The pharmaceutical companies get a kick back, there are three hundred people at MacDougal's and they are all on one kind of narcotic or another. It kept us pliable, controllable. I was getting prescribed 120 mg/day, a common dose for terminally ill cancer patients, to sedate and make them comfortable on their way out. A typical dose for a burn survivor is 40 to 60 mg/day.

There were suicide attempts: hoarding my oxy and drinking a fifth of Jack Daniels, ending in being found by a nurse assistant close to dead. Twice. There would have been more had it not been for my daughter.

For a long while after the incident I dealt with severe feelings of isolation. I was the only one that was in the coma; my scars freaked people out. I'd never met another burn survivor with burns as severe as mine until 2008 when I met Mona and Alisa at Portland Burn Survivors. Mona was burned in a car accident thirty years ago and has injuries more severe than mine. Yet she was living an independent and happy life. In 2009 we attended the World Burn Congress in New York run by the Phoenix Society. I had an opportunity to see that my disfigurement was not all that bad. I met hundreds of burn survivors who had sustained injuries like mine and were thriving. I was lucky to be alive. I guess. But I was wrapped up in the Oxycotin, Valium and pot cookie cocktails they fed me at MacDougal's. They were all prescribed so I didn't give it a second thought. I'd look in the mirror at the top of my head and the severity of the injury wouldn't register because I was so heavily medicated. I knew what I was doing but did it anyway. I realized I'd been hiding in another drug-induced coma for the past five years. I had to get clean and start advocating for myself.

I told them I wanted out. After the initial meeting, it only took a month to get out of MacDougal's and into Unthank Plaza. Unthank

Alisa and Paul

Plaza is a hands-off, low-income apartment complex. The contrast was stark. Once out of MacDougal's I was cut off from narcotics sending me into a spell of intense withdrawals. It was terrible. All of the sudden they take it away and I was a mess. Had the system backed me with occupational therapy, or at least tapered me off opiates, I would have been much more self-sufficient. I had been doped quiet at The MacDougal's house; I didn't realize how much until I was on my own without narcotics. Unthank Plaza was too hands off, I stayed for just a few months and then moved to Elderly Village which is more of an assisted living facility.

Foot Drop is a phenomenon that happens to a lot of stroke patients. It can be corrected by a cast or brace to gradually bring the foot back up to a normal direction. While I was in the old folk's home, they gave no cast, no brace and no therapy for drop foot. It continued to droop and distort until it was a twisted gnarl and I as unable to walk. They gave me an electric wheelchair (about $6,000) which I did not ask for. I don't know how much the federal government and the producer of the motorized wheel chair got from the deal but I refused it. They were forced to look at my foot. It had been looked at by a foot doctor at Emanuel—he stated nothing could be done except put it in a brace. I could walk but the brace was ill-fitting, incredibly painful and cumbersome. It rubbed away skin to form calices and blisters. I was stuck with that brace for years. Of course if I had the right insurance I would have been a lot further along than I am now. Just this past summer, ten years later, I finally found a doctor at Providence to perform the foot surgery. He put two screws in my foot so it sits straight. There was a two week recovery after that the cast was off. Two and a half months later, I'm walking. Now I can wear my boots.

All in all I felt very unsupported by the medical industry. For example, a doctor that I'm seeing now changes my medication as he sees fit without consulting me or asking for my input. I had an inhaler that worked very well for me; I could use it twice a day and be good to go. He then put me on two different inhalers, neither of which I could operate. After two weeks of complaining, he finally listened to me. I have extremely limited finger use and could not operate them. He switched my prescription back.

Another complication is navigating the insurance companies. I have had several skin graph surgeries for my head and face; however I need skin graphs for the area surrounding my eyes. That is qualified as 'cosmetic' by insurance companies. I need it to close my eyes— that is not cosmetic - that is insane. I am not a socialite.

The doctors at Emanuel wouldn't perform the surgery so I went to the eye doctors at Good Samaritan who referred me to a surgeon at OHSU. He wasn't as scared of the insurance company—he graphed underneath my left eyelid this past September. My right eyelid will be done in December. This is care that I would have never gotten had I not advocated for myself and gone through three different hospitals. I understand I wasn't an angel before or after the fire but I still deserve care.

I am still at Elderly Village. They are helping with the PTSD, because mentally I am still disturbed. Ten years feels like yesterday sometimes. It's nice to have solitude. If I choose to have a couple of beers, they will leave me alone. As a recovering drug addict and alcoholic I've reached a place that I am a functioning alcoholic. I drink a couple of beers a week and smoke a little pot. I'm finding out pot is very helpful to reduce the stress.

Now I'm going to be a granddad! I'm so blown out. I like that my daughter has found a guy who is real good with her; she was in a bad living situation when she was sixteen. Jonathan got her out of that environment and they are still together. I have nothing bad to say about him, I am so grateful for him getting her out of that mess.

My daughter is a big part of my life and has been for a long time. There would have been several more suicide attempts had it not been for the forethought of my daughter being out a dad. The idea of me getting on a plane and going to see all of them by myself—that's in the cards . . .

A phone call from her saying she loves me makes it worth it.

Labonya Siddique

Labonya Siddique

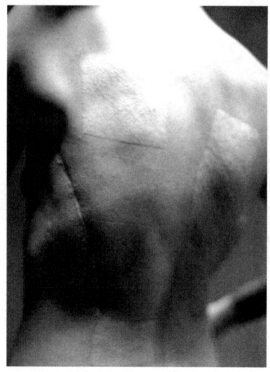

Alisa before, spring 2001, and after, spring 2003

Alisa Christensen

I was injured at the end of 2001; 40% 3rd and 4th degree burns from a camping accident and brain damage from a stroke while under anesthesia (I agree with Paul Peterson, brain damage is far worse to navigate and live with than my burn injury). I lost most of the functional use of my right arm and hand, my dominant hand.

I'd always been artistic and athletic pre-injury. I was a stunt double in Los Angeles, flew trapeze, danced until dawn on the weekends, rode my mountain bike up the canyons, liked yoga. My parents were really into the arts and as a child I took classical piano from age of five to twelve. I also played guitar, liked sing along and liked to draw and paint. After the fire, I stopped all of these activities; some I obviously had no choice but others, because I found it less painful to learn new things, than to do badly what I used to do easily.

A few years of healing go by and I finally had the itch to create again. I started with web design and nude photography (CafeDeb and The Naked Man), which was a blast and gave me confidence. I wrote a memoir, *gimp surviving your survival*, five years after the fire (soon to be released as *gimp 2.0*). I moved on to mixed media collages of my pill bottles, which turned into collages of other things, found objects mostly. I realized I could find artistic satisfaction in many different ways; it didn't have to be two-handed activities. Just do it.

'Orange Pills' by Alisa Christensen

'Mouse Train' by Alisa Christensen

The Rhythm of Life

By Betsy Pucci Stemple

I have been in three of the world's most well known cities: London, Paris and New York. Each of them has a kind of reputation for the locals being rude. I had a different perspective on this after a trip to London with my kids.

We were traveling on the tube. It was morning; people were going to work or coming home from work. Lots of people. Lots and lots of people. The underground tunnels are like a huge maze of shiny white tile and benches. Many of the benches are constructed so one cannot lie down and sleep on them. There are gourmet coffee shops, cheese shops, restaurants and even clothing stores and salons. Some kiosks appear to be built in such a way that commuters need only slow their pace to grab something and catch the next train. There is a real pattern and rhythm to their movement.

While we were changing trains my nine year old son, David, slipped or stopped or something. I don't remember what happened; only the affect it had on the rhythm. A few people behind him had to slow down, one had to step around him. The initial look on their faces was one of exasperation or anger followed quickly by the realization that it was just a kid. He didn't know the rules or the dance yet so it was OK for him to be out of step. Had David been an adult I am sure he would have felt as though the folks giving him a dirty look were rude.

After all, he had just messed up the pulse of the London Underground. The constant flow and pace that everyone was able to maintain was challenged. People who do that always seem to get our scorn. A person too slow in traffic gets the finger. I have often shot daggers at someone in the grocery store who wants to run back for an item they forgot while they are in the middle of checking out. In

Minnesota, you shouldn't walk up the middle of the sledding hill. It messes up the rhythm.

Over ten years ago now my friend Alisa was injured in a tragic accident. During her multiple surgeries and treatments she also suffered a stroke. She is physically disabled and has some residual effects from the stroke that involve her word-finding ability. The stroke as has also compromised her ability to regulate her emotional response to certain situations.

I remember one of the first times we ventured out together after the accident. She was staying with her folks in northern Minnesota. She and I and my two kids went to a small aquarium in Duluth, Minnesota. Alisa was still in a wheelchair. Sometimes I pushed her, sometimes the kids did and sometimes she wheeled herself. I found myself getting frustrated  with our pace through the aquarium. I had a schedule in my head of when we would finish and when we would eat, or when we could get back to the hotel and the kids could swim. Part way through the aquarium I had to tell myself to just knock it off. We were out having fun and looking at things. The kids were fine; I was shamed by their ease to lean on the wheel chair or fight over who got to push it. They were just being in the time and space around them. Just adjusting to the rhythm.

I think of having a handicapped friend like learning a new dance or new way of moving through the world, especially when you have the other version of the person in your mind. You are used to being one way with them and now you have to change.

I have had the unfortunate experience of being with Alisa when folks around us just couldn't adjust to our slower rhythm. There was a woman who began making loud sighing noises behind us in a store when Alisa was trying to get change out of her purse. At a large renaissance festival in Minnesota, a woman called her a "fucking bitch" in a crowd of people because Alisa couldn't move her cane and bag where this woman wanted. I lost my mind and made a spectacle of myself yelling at this woman. Sometimes it reminds me of a pack of animals trying to cull a weaker member of the heard. It's bizarre. As if her disability was contagious.

When I am with Alisa I slow down, we sit longer in restaurants, we watch the kids longer at the park. Our slow walk on the Oregon shore where we were able to take in the cliffs and the houses and the waves and the large rocks out in the ocean was magical. I might have just been thinking about the next place without the time being somehow slowed down. We are sort of in a different place. Either unseen by other because we just sit there and go so slow or perhaps more visible because they wonder why we are so slow.

It was a great tragedy for my friend to be so hurt. It has been a life lesson and a blessing to me to maintain the friendship. I am challenged to be a new kind of person. I am someone accepting and patient, someone just being in the now. I hate that phrase but it really sort of fits. I hope my friendship to her has been as valuable as hers is to me.

Fading at just under the speed limit before living again as a Story in an imaging.
Chago Roberto DeSantiago

When I am found lifeless body less I will never say that I have been murdered remembering my suicides I will only recall what I have survived and the great music that was played.
Chago Roberto DeSantiago

My Story

By Chris Backer

When I was eighteen, I began having issues with my health: cramps, diarrhea and a lot of pain. I saw the doctor, who sent me to a specialist, who loved to do scopes. He told me that it looked like I had Crohn's disease. Blood work and a few other tests confirmed his diagnosis. I was immediately put on steroids. For the most part things went well, except for my mind. I felt like I was going nuts. I felt too good, which resulted from some "over the top" behavior.

When the steroids stopped working, or between courses of them, I was introduced to a number of other medications from Percocet, to antidiarrhetics. All were supposed to help, but many only made things worse. At about this point, without warning my specialist moved to the States. After three years and without transferring my rather large file. I was sent to another specialist at the hospital who didn't know me and had to establish a new file. I was run through a myriad of tests, looking for everything from Lupus to Lycanthropes. I was sent to one doctor who put me on elimination diets in the hopes of pinpointing a particular food as the culprit. I was made to eat baby food, to eliminate thorough chewing as an issue. You name it, I tried it, or stopped trying it. Nothing they recommended helped.

Onto another specialist and Crohn's was again the culprit. So back to steroids I went. After a year with this new specialist, he retired. I got another new specialist, who (you guessed it) ran his own list of tests. He had some new medicines to try that I hadn't heard of yet. Almost all of them landed me in hospital or at the very least, sick at home. He and I didn't get along very well. Half the medicines he prescribed aren't even on the market anymore. I just couldn't keep eating all those pills. After a year or so with him, I got sent to another specialist so we didn't have to deal with each other anymore. The new specialist did the

123

scopes at the hospital; after a particularly bad experience during a scope, panicking, they held me down choking on the camera, I got sent to another specialist.

This was a great doctor and he helped for the first time in my life. He took me off pain pills and introduced me to immunosuppressant. However after a few years on them I started to develop some side effects. I wound up getting warts. Everywhere. I couldn't get rid of them fast enough and that meant having them burned off or cut out at the hospital. Some days I had to leave the hospital on crutches to mind the holes they cut in my feet. I couldn't take it anymore and chose to stop the immunosuppressant. It took five more years before the warts finally stopped. That's five more years of freezing and cutting. During this time I began to speak to my new doctor about marijuana instead of the other drugs. He didn't know enough about it to have an opinion and he would retire in another couple years, so no progress there.

Now we're on to my current specialist, whom I cherish dearly. I feel she really cares about how I feel. This doctor agreed to sign my exemption for medical marijuana and I was on my way to better health, safely. I had already been using cannabis before I stopped using the immunosuppressant. It has been eight years that I've been self-medicating with cannabis. During this time I came across www.phoenixtears.ca, a website that showed the benefits of cannabis oil, as opposed to the whole plant. So I don't have to smoke it? Awesome. By making and eating the oil, I've been able to control my own health for six years now with my new doctor. If you're counting, that's fourteen years of cannabis, the last twelve being cannabis only. No other pills. Period.

So here we are now; I'm legal to use marijuana but not the oil. I can't eat the plant cause it hurts but the oil works great. I eat it daily and no longer get "high" from it. But like possessing it, manufacturing the oil is also illegal and dangerous. Once while making my medicine, as I'd done hundreds of other times, something went wrong. The rice cooker I was using sparked and started a fire. In trying to get the fire out, it spilled over me, first setting my arms on fire. As I continued to try and get the fire out things kept getting worse. I ran outside fully engulfed in blue flames to a patch of grass to "stop, drop and roll." As I rolled back and forth, I was out, on, out, on, out, after finally rolling in one direction.

Someone jumped the fence into my yard to help try and put me out but he wasn't able to help, the rolling did it. There was more alcohol in the house that I had to get out to avoid an explosion and four dogs I had to find. I went back in four times to get everything. The dogs were fine. When the ambulance showed up, I was sitting on the front doorstep exhausted, in my half burnt drawers, still on fire. I remember yelling as they took me away, "where's the fire truck?" The pain was horrible on the way in and it took forever to get there. They asked a million questions that I couldn't concentrate on. I think I remember arriving at the hospital but that's it until I woke up from a coma with a tube in my throat three days later.

They didn't think I'd make it and had to medicate my wife before they'd let her see me. The next thing I remember was the nightmares, or dreams, or hallucinations. Whatever you want to call them, they were insane. Not knowing what's real or not. Not being able to speak or move to express yourself is its own nightmare. People tried to communicate but eventually would leave me there with these horrible people that were torturing me. I even tried to kick a nurse in the head twice, I thought he was going to sell me to some Nigerian guy to be hunted for sport (I know but it seemed real; don't judge me, lol). They had to tie me down for a bit.

I tried to cry out for them to stay but they left anyway, promising to come back tomorrow and me not knowing if I'd still be there tomorrow. But I was, if only so the nightmares could begin again. They went on for an entire month. The day they let me have marijuana brought to me in hospital was the last nightmare I had.

They stopped instantly. It was a battle for access but as a legal patient I was permitted to have edibles brought to me daily. As long it was brought by another legal patient and my pain med doses were adjusted to account for the marijuana. Beyond the burns, I also suffered a double pulmonary embolism and a stroke that took the vision from my left eye. Add to that a bout of shingles, MRSA and Pseudomonas in the hospital and you begin to see how amazing it is to still be here. The doctors put a temporary filter in my chest to catch blot clots but then forgot it there. Now it's permanent, as are the blood thinners I have to take daily because of it.

Over the next seven months, as I healed and learned to walk again, the nurses and doctors became aware of the incredible healing properties of cannabis. They have all stated that I healed at least 40% faster than any other burn patients they had ever seen. After being burned 2nd and 3rd degree on over 85% of my body and four months in a hospital bed, intensive physiotherapy and occupational therapy got me up so I could march my ass out to the arcade for the sweetest joint I've ever smoked.

From that point on, they couldn't stop me from walking. They could barely keep me in my room. I excelled in my therapy and they were constantly amazed by my progress. Every day is an incredible gift when you're not supposed to be here anymore. I see some people look, or stare but I don't care. What other people think of you is none of your business (that's an adage I prescribe to). I had one lady look at me in the hospital, as she held the elevator for me, she said, " . . . you TRY and have a nice day." I suppose I'll have to do just that, just like everyone else.

Artists' Bios

Rob Bispo / Salem, Oregon, USA

I was at a yoga studio recently in Portland. I wore a long sleeved UnderArmour winter shirt. The room must've been at least 90° and was getting hot quick. I wanted to take my shirt off; it felt like I was going to suffocate. Although I've seen men take their shirts off in yoga classes, I didn't want to be the first. So when another man took his shirt off, I thought what the heck, here goes my shirt. I don't look burned with clothes on. With all the noise that was going on, the room went silent. And I was all good with that, I'm used to it. I see myself from the inside. Then we all went to the locker room. I remember about six men in a small space. No matter which way I turned I could see and feel someone trying to get a look at my skin. Again I'm not uncomfortable just a bit annoyed that no one would ask me what happened. Wtf. Even at a freak show people are allowed to ask questions. I am quite comfortable in my skin. Please ask me questions any time.
Namaste, YogiRob.org

Mona Krueger / Lake Oswego, Oregon, USA

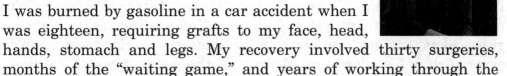

I consider myself a wannabe author, volunteer social worker and organized pile-buster. After-care for burn and trauma survivors matters to me. I love traveling, an ocean view, football and fru-fru coffee. I self-published my memoir last year, *Sage Was The Perfect Shadow*, and write a blog for survivors: monakrueger.com.

I was burned by gasoline in a car accident when I was eighteen, requiring grafts to my face, head, hands, stomach and legs. My recovery involved thirty surgeries, months of the "waiting game," and years of working through the grief to reestablish my identity and find new meaning in life. My faith played a huge role in the process.

I learn so much from other survivors. Together we can keep perspective and persevere on this journey—the camaraderie of a shared reality is truly powerful.

Marty Lupoli / Salem, Oregon, USA

I was burned in an electrical fire in 2009. Over 70% of my body. Tough to take but I didn't let it stop me for long. I keep busy with friends, gardening, carving and painting walking sticks and tools; I get unconditional love and support from my mom and brother. I'm happy to be alive.

Jamie Uttley / Manchester, Lancashire, U.K

I am currently still taking things slow and easy; trying to get back into work courses for the future. I can say that now I have the ability to overcome anything that comes into my way. Not as easily but all the support I have around me is marvelous. I have a few decent friends I can rely on. Most of all I'm in touch and living strong with my family again, helping other survivors as I go.

Website, jamieuttley.moonfruit.com

Ibrahim Mubarak and Lisa Fay / Portland, Oregon, USA

I was burned at eight years old, my wife was fifteen, but we didn't meet for another thirty years. I started 'Right 2 Survive' in 2009, a grass roots activist organization to protect the rights of people experiencing homelessness. At about the same time, Lisa was working with another activist group 'Phoenix Rising' and we met.

We had similar interests and a lot in common, we were soon dating and got married two and a half years ago.

We met Trevor and Alisa at one of our meetings and they came to one of our direct action's 'Pitch A Tent,' protesting how Portland allows housed people to pitch a tent for the fun of watching a parade but won't allow houseless people to camp within the city for survival. After that fun night we all became friends, went to the Rainbow Gathering and started another direct action in October 2011, 'Right 2 Dream, too' (R2Dtoo), a rest area for people without permanent housing on Burnside and 4th. Alisa gave us her book to read; we realized that we were both burn survivors too, although we hadn't thought about it for years. We think getting injured that young did alter the paths of our lives. We experienced pain and fear, hiding our scars and being afraid of what other people would think. I hope it's helped us to always be supportive of our disabled brothers and sisters, and think it added strength to our characters.

Email, i_tpop@hotmail.com

Labonya Siddique / Burnley, Lancashire, UK

I was rescued by my mother and admitted into the hospital with 40% second-degree, full thickness burns across the front, underarms, face and in patches across the legs. After a five day comatose state, I woke with amnesia even when doctors declared me least likely to survive the first night. For two years I was treated with silicone treatment and pressure garments.

Thankfully we escaped the social stigma in Bangladesh and came to England. But that did not put an end to the troubles ahead. My entire teens and adolescent years comprised of PTSD-related depression, episodic panic attacks, night terror and self-harm. Since the day I woke up in hospital, I wanted to die every day, every night wishing it was my last. The shame, the guilt, the self-hate, the ugliness I had become. I hid for years, dwelled alone for countless nights. Sometimes in life, you are hit with so many disasters and obstacles you eventually get tired of being the victim.

And start to fight back, you stop caring about what the world thinks and instead focus on how you feel, what you need to achieve and what you want to become. I am beautiful because deep down, for me beauty comes from a feeling. What I went through taught me how important it is to use every possible way to spread this message of confidence to every man and woman, scarred or not—never surrender, never regret, never give up and never feel any less than you know you are worth.

Kelly Falardeau / Stony Plain, Alberta, Canada

I became a burn survivor when I was two years old on 75% of my body. I constantly struggled with my self-worth and confidence and never thought I would find a husband or have kids, but I did. I found a way to go from near-death to success; from the ugly scar-faced girl to the Top 10 Most Powerful and Influential Speakers, Fierce Woman of the Year, three time Best-Selling Author, recipient of the Queen Elizabeth II Diamond Jubilee Medal and most recently a YWCA Woman of Distinction. You have to ask yourself how? How did a burn survivor who constantly struggled with rejection, staring and teasing burst through all the negativity in her life to succeed? I wrote three books, *No Risk No Rewards*, *'Self-Esteem Doesn't Come in a Bottle*, and *'1000 Tips for Teenagers*, all are available on my website, KellyFalardeau.com.

Email, mykellyf@gmail.com

Mark McEachren / Grand Canyon, Arizona, USA

I consider myself a poet-philosopher. I like that combination; a creative, colorful, dreamer that loves practical application and deep thought. Everyone has his or her approach and view of life; every path is different. All I know is I'm in it for the experience. Not some collection of decaying tokens and monuments. This

story is proof that experiences can live on, continually finding new life. What could be cooler than that?

- Mark W. McEachren (AKA The Naked Man)
Email, mceachrenmark@aol.com

Nancy Tran / Orange, California, USA

Becoming a burn survivor was never something I have ever imagined myself to be. Although it is one of the most painful and horrendous traumas to endure, I have also had many great opportunities and magical moments that I would have never imagined. I am a 32 year old woman, Vietnamese-American born and currently going to grad school pursuing my Master's of Social Work concentrating in mental health and sub-concentrating in military social work. I will be done with the master's program on August, 2014

in hopes of working with veterans. I am currently living in Orange, CA and living life to the fullest. Support and unconditional love from my family and friends has helped me thrive; to become the woman I have always wanted to be. I am someone who is independent, strong, loving and gives back to the community since they have put so much time for me. Paying it forward is my absolute motto and I will continue to assist those in need for those to live a good quality life.

Email, nancy.t.tran@gmail.com

Carmen Barker / Sylmar, California, USA

Hello I'm 26 years old and have been a burn survivor as of May 10, 2011. I had a car accident and was burned 45% along with multiple fractures. My poem is about all of the obstacles I went through and am still going through to this day. I had a lot to deal with all at once after my accident; getting dumped, being separated from my son, dealing with what I looked like. Then I began getting adjusted and becoming independent as much as possible.

Email, krocks712@gmail.com.

Kenneth G. Alvis / Portland, Oregon, USA

I was working as a millwright's apprentice at a nickel smelting operation located in Southern Oregon. The accident ignited my work coveralls. The date was January 26th 1991. I was 31 years old with 87% body burns. Life flight flew me to the Burn Center located in Portland Oregon.

Five months later I was released into the real world of therapy, family and all the challenges that come with reintegration as a burn survivor. My son was now nearly a year old. The two daughters were seven and twelve years old at the time of my hospital release.

Both daughters are parents now. The "boy" attends Community College. It was only with the support of many fine people and the committed staff of the Oregon Burn Unit that I was able to raise those children into the wonderful adults and parents they are today.

I enjoy gardening and riding my motorcycle. I attempt to create art in a variety of mediums. As illustrated in *"...do I believe?" stories and art by survivors*, my success is dubious. Creating is still an exciting and rewarding experience and for me adds depth and meaning to life beyond the survivor experience.

Donna Bailey / Durham, Hartlepoole, UK

I live in a small town in North East England, UK. I studied psychology at the University of York and graduated with a BSc Honors. Post graduation, I took several positions as an assistant psychologist before changing direction and gaining a position as an Emergency Planning Officer for the year 2000 project. I was then successful at getting a permanent job as an Emergency Planning Officer and was quickly promoted to Senior Civil Contingency Planning Officer with added responsibility for Business Continuity Planning. I worked with a multitude of organizations from local authorities to the Emergency Services and Public Health professionals writing and testing emergency and business continuity plans and responding to local emergencies.

I never realized when a nurse in the burns unit in 2007 said, " . . . if you get back to work," that my burns would prevent me from working! I thought I would come out of hospital and be 'fixed,' what was she talking about? 'If . . . '. How wrong I was. There were many things I'd never thought about— just took them for granted—walking, using both hands, daily living and bathing to name just a few. The frustrations still exist but I am trying to make the best of things (most of the time.) I get a lot of help  particularly from my amazing mum who continues to be my brick and my best friend. I am so lucky to still have her and my brother for love, support and encouragement and I am sure my dad still gives me this too even though he is no longer physically with us.

I am currently finalizing two distant learning courses in Crystal Healing and Colour Therapy and hope someday in some way I can go back to my psychology roots. The future is scary but I am determined to continue to find solutions to the barriers I face.

Kim Dormier / Reedville, Oregon, USA

This is my story of personal hope beyond tragedy. I was born in Odessa, Texas and lived my early life in Southeast Idaho. I have resided in Oregon the past seventeen years and have made a career working for an international microchip fabrication company. I am the mother of two, a grandmother of two and am active in the music and teaching ministry of my church.

I am the survivor of a burn victim. Though I don't suffer the physical and lasting scars of being a burn survivor, I've endured the emotional scars of losing my father as a burn victim. The pain and suffering due to third degree burns over 60% of his body lasted six weeks but the emotional pain of a little girl losing her father will last a lifetime. I will always remember the day I saw my dad all wrapped up in loose bandages, only seeing the bright red tips of his fingers as he lay there helpless. He only wanted to give his little girl a kiss goodbye. My memories of him as a man and father will remain with me always, as well as the last moments I saw him.

Email, Kad2855@comcast.net

George Goodwin / Reno, Nevada, USA

My full name is George A. Goodwin III but you can call me George. I live in Reno, Nevada (USA) but was burned after being hit by a drunken driver while in Japan. I was burned in August, 2004 with 60% TBSA and 2nd and 3rd degree burns. I returned to the U.S., and though I started a degree in Journalism, I switched to Public Health after finding out that there was no burn ward in Northern Nevada. I am about to receive my MPH (Master's Degree in Public Health) from the University of Nevada, Reno and though I don't have a job to speak of, I have had quite a few adventures over the last six years or so. I interned in a Congressman's office, went to China to perform a study in a burn ward in Beijing and I've spent countless hours in the library.

I've had mixed results from people regarding my burns. Nevada has one of the loveliest sunsets that you could possibly see in your life—easily comparable to anything offered in Hawaii—but the people here are mixed. There are those who are kind, who smile and hold no grudges but likewise there are those who try to make you feel as if your very presence seems to diminish their own sense  of well-being. These latter folks can be very hard on burn survivors as they often take the attitude that anyone or anything less than perfect that dares exist within presence of their line of sight needs to be dismissed or somehow cleared away post-haste. I certainly have a love-hate relationship with this city and its people.

Email, notsosurearewe@hotmail.com

Clare Latchem / Devon, Sidmouth, UK

I currently live in a small seaside town called Sidmouth; it is located in the south west of the United Kingdom. This hasn't always been my main place of residence and I think I must have been a gypsy in a past life! My family immigrated to New Zealand when I was nine. I spent the rest of my childhood and early teenage years growing up there before returning back to the UK in 1987. Since then I have moved around quite a lot and love to travel whenever I can.

My burns have definitely stifled my growth as a person and I am still trying to overcome that. The irony of my affliction is that I love the water; I love to swim and love the oceans. I am a keen scuba diver but revealing my scars to the public eye is a battle for me and this is something I still have to try and combat.

I have currently been studying environmental conservation and have a particular interest in marine conservation. I would love to try and progress my learning or career in this area; however, competition is fierce and jobs are few and far between. So I am now about to embark on a counseling course to keep me stimulated and maybe I can put this education and my life experiences to positive use, helping others overcome difficulties their in life.

I have the most amazing family and friends in which I love dearly and they have all been so supportive throughout some extremely harrowing and emotional times with me.

Email, clarelatchem@yahoo.co.uk

Yolonda Hawkins / Los Angeles, California, USA

At age 28 I became involved in a burn support group at The Grossman Burn Center and then started volunteering on the burn unit. I talk and help new burn patients to eat and show them that their life is not over just because they were burned. Volunteering and helping burn survivors has become my passion in life.

I am now 42 and have been with my boyfriend for about five years. We planned and finally had a son named Aiden in February 2013. Life is great! I believe we all are given tests in life that teach us how strong we really are.

Email, amuzeme@aol.com

Laura Brixey / Beaverton, Oregon, USA

I was born and grew up in Montana. After graduating high school, I moved to North Carolina where I met and married my first husband. Two years later, I gave birth to my one and only child, Brenda. I completed my third year at UNCW. I was very active in my church in North Carolina where I was on the jail ministry team, interpreting and teaching a signing class, sang in the choir, began the hospitality committee, coordinated the church thanksgiving dinner for about 300 people, was active in the women's ministry and various children's ministries.

When the marriage ended in disaster, I moved to the Portland area to be close to my family. There I completed my degree in elementary education at PSU and worked as a substitute teacher in the surrounding area for ten years. I involved myself in raising my daughter, friends, family, church and teaching in the church, mainly children (even adults one summer).

After fifteen years I met and married the love of my life. We enjoy a simple but busy life together. I continue to be active in my church, working in various departments, mostly teaching children. Richard and I continue to be involved with the burn support group. I enjoy being a Nana to seven grandchildren at this time.

Richard was born in Alaska where he spent most of his childhood. He left Alaska to attend college in Oregon, eventually graduating from PSU. Except for a short return to Alaska, he remained in Oregon. Richard continues to be active in church and at work. He still plants a good-sized garden every spring. He jogs every other day. We attend the Portland Burn Survivors support group. When we are called, we visit others who are in the hospital.

All totaled, Richard spent five weeks in the hospital and two weeks in rehab. He returned to work four months almost to the day. He lost his left arm and three toes, the first two on the right foot and the pinky toe on the left food. Not bad for such a mishap as this!

Trevor Beam / Longview, Washington, USA

For the past few years I've been working at Napa Auto Parts store, I like it. Since finding other burn survivors I went to the World Burn Congress in Galveston in 2010; it was the first time I'd ever seen so many survivors together and we had a great time. Portland, OR has a rose parade every spring and the city lets people camp downtown to reserve a place for the parade. In spring of 2011, we were looking on facebook for something to do and saw a protest for the homeless about camping. PDX doesn't allow camping the other 364 days a year, so we went down to join the protest and made a bunch of great friends from Right 2 Survive.

The Rainbow Gathering was just a few weeks away and so Alisa and I went with nine of our new friends. The Rainbow Gathering was started in the 70's as a way to say welcome home to Vietnam veterans. I put on my dog suit and barked at a vet. I have a dog; he's a good dog, a thirteen-year-old Boston Bull Terrier. (He doesn't like cats—he chases them.) I drove to Southern Oregon to go and get him just after my accident. I am lucky to have my two older sisters and my mom. The injury was more than ten years ago so I am able to look back at it with time-tempered judgment.

Sara McIlroy / Spokane, Washington, USA

I was burned in February 2013. I was cooking and sauce boiled over onto the stove. I leaned down to clean it up, my hair was very long and caught on the burner. I had hairspray in my bangs which caused my hair to blow up. I didn't know how badly I was burned until the next day, I just thought I'd lost all of my hair. The next morning I was in pain and my mom took me to the ER; they figured I was in shock the night before.

They wanted to medivac me to Harborview Medical Center in Seattle, Washington but I didn't have insurance so told them no. My mom took me the 4 ½ hour drive. I had 3rd degree burns and was hospitalized for a month and a half. I had three surgeries for skin grafts. I burnt the left side of my face, my neck, the left side of my chest, shoulder and armpit.

It has been a real struggle for me. I'm scarred, I lost all my hair but it has been gradually growing back and I wear a wig. I had to find t-shirts that were high enough to cover the scars both on my chest and arms because summer was coming. In summer I couldn't go outside when it was hot because I was very sensitive to heat (which the staff warned me about).

Now with winter coming I have to find high neck shirts to cover my scars. I have been very self-conscious and feel like Frankenstein sewn back together. I have been struggling with depression, thoughts of suicide and feeling like I will never be whole again. I was considered an attractive woman, now I feel like half a woman. Though the doctors say I am healing very well, I look at my scars and think they must be crazy. I thought I would be normal in a year, now I know it will take years before the scars really fade. I am often depressed and frustrated daily so I have sought counseling to help me cope with my feelings; try to accept the new me.

I am planning on returning to work and need to find work clothes that cover my scars. All of my current work clothes show neck and chest scars. It is a constant struggle dealing with the aftermath of being burned and I don't think anyone really understands until it has happened to them.

AnnMarie Balik / Thermopolis, Wyoming, USA

I survived a serious burn injury at the tender age of seven while helping with care taking duties in a Catholic Church. I underwent an extensive hospitalization which included continuous blood transfusions and nearly daily skin grafts.

During my young twenties, I had more energy and inspiration and completed two cross country bicycle tours (Seattle to Boston and Canada to California). I also had the energy and initiative to backpack solo in Europe and on the Lake Superior Hiking Trail in Northern Minnesota.

As an adult I have worked in roles as an elementary teacher, occupational therapist, yoga instructor and shaman. Currently, I prefer a low stress life and enjoy having fun with various activities of artwork, creative writing, yoga and spending time in nature. Currently I reside in the rural State of Wyoming and vacation a great deal in California to spend time on the beach. I'm thinking that I would like to re-locate to California.

Over the course of my life, I have been a healing junkie. Through various alternative methods of healing, I have finally gotten relief from PTSD which had ruled my life for years. Various healing techniques utilized have included: chiropractic, acupuncture, nutrition, hypnotherapy, massage, counseling, art, cranio-sacral, radionics, shaman energy medicine, neuro feedback, yoga, meditation, EMDR, deep yogic breathing, Reiki, flower essences, tapping, visualization, touch for health and likely other methods that I have not thought of while writing this biography.

Finding the PBSurvivors.org on the internet has provided the first type of burn survivor support that I have ever experienced. I have found the group to be very supportive and knowledgeable of the deep trauma experienced by burn survivors.

Email, h2yoga@hotmail.com

Chago Robert DeSantiago / Sylmar, California, USA

I still have both of my parents; I have a younger sister and a younger brother. I am the oldest grandchild on both sides of my family. I would say that I am an aspiring artist but really I am just trying to find ways to express all of that which I feel in a positive manner that helps me to cope and hopefully helps others as well. My primary expressions are in writing and photography and I hope to try painting soon.

Under our sinks and through out our homes we have a specialized chemicals to clean just about every single thing in the very same house. My story starts out when I am fifteen months old. I decided I had a clogged throat and got the Drano out from under the bathroom sink and proceeded to pour it down into my clogged throat. It gets kind of black after that last part and after thirty-seven years, I still do not remember if it worked on my clogged throat or not so you are going to have to live with the mystery just as I am. I would tell you not to try  this at home though and if you have kids, or other people's kids that visit your house often then you should safeguard your sinks and other places where household chemicals are kept.

It is hard to believe that an adult would hurt a child intentionally, especially without any proof. If you have a mind that loves to block out moments of extreme pain in your life, maybe that's a good thing. I have been wanting to do some sort of experiment to see how quickly acid burns flesh and bone. It may involve a complete cow's head with tongues and everything still inside of it. I will wet the inside of the head down with water and then pour in the Drano (same formula from the seventies would be ideal it was the most potent) watch it burn for a few minutes, then pour in some milk like they did with me and check out the damage. No, I would not think of doing this to a live animal. I have got to check myself sometimes, lest I would get some bad ideas, best to cast them out as soon as they form rather then let them fester in the subconscious mind. I should add I would never think of doing this to another human being either. I assume that the smell alone would be one of the most horrible smells I have ever had the displeasure of smelling but it would be second to the smell of my own burning mouth; that is all I would have to be able see if I could jog the fuck out of some of my repressed memories. I know they are there stored waiting for me to figure out how to unlock them I am hoping that smell will do this for me. It has to actually since I don't have the screams of a burning child, or my own pain to help me out with this.

I would say I have sight too but I am pretty sure I did not get to see the insides of my mouth burning, so the sight would not be of much use to me and I sure as hell am not going to go with the taste again. You know I have used Drano repeatedly since my accident and the smell of it has yet to bring back any repressed childhood traumaries (memories+ trauma=traumaries).

So that is pretty much me in a nutshell. I am currently working on building a small shed which will be half storage and half studio to hopefully start producing my works with the intent of sales. I have also been in therapy for the first time, ironically it was not being able to ship fotos that clients want to purchase that lead me in to therapy and not what I have gone through with my burns. I would like to thank Portland Burn Survivors, Inc for this wonderful opportunity to share my life and living with you all and I hope that you enjoy.

Peace, Love and Light be with you all.

Bethany Storro / Vancouver, Washington, USA

On August 20th 2010 I did the unthinkable, dousing my own face with acid in a suicide attempt that failed. Trying to hide from the truth, I told lies that became national news. My journey started with an elaborate maze of mental illness leading up to the tragedy. I wrote a book in 2012 outlining the events. My desire is that others facing similar paths will find help and hope before dire consequences  ensue. *Facing the Truth.* is an honest look at the underpinnings of the rare body dismorphic disorder (BDD) and its long-term effects.

Email, besstinamove@gmail.com.

Paul Peterson / Portland, Oregon, USA

All upper body: head and throat, about 30% was burned. Before my injury, for my living I was a temp. I was a member of the Oregon National Guard in the early 80's. I always loved reading and riding my bike. If I wasn't already reading a book I would be looking for a book. The bicycle was a way to travel. If you travel by train or bus, you're just 'that homeless guy.' When you have a bicycle: you are a cyclist. Go to Montana for a summer, Sacramento for a winter. After the injury, being unable to travel was a huge contributing factor to feeling so depressed and suicidal. This is the longest time I've had to stay in one place.

I can no longer read (because of my eyesight) so I am very grateful for audio books. I'm undergoing laser eye surgery in early December, and hopefully will be reading after that. If I hadn't been an alcoholic or was an 'upstanding citizen' with good insurance, I would have been treated very differently. The physicians and doctors at Emanuel seem to have no empathy. The doctors at Good Sam's and Providence are willing to put forth the effort and it's appreciated. . I am thankful for the support I get from April, my mother and brother. I've been fortunate to have found comfort in a compassionate, loving network of fellow burn survivors.

Alisa Christensen / Portland, Oregon, USA

I went into the operating room expecting to wake in about forty-five minutes. The USC staff decided to keep changing my right arm under sedation. They'd tried it while I was awake a couple days earlier, just turned up my morphine drip. I screamed in agony while a burn surgeon showed a group of interns how well I was healing. They had to tie my arm down. It was creepy cool to see healthy red tissue around bright white bone (you're not supposed to see your own bones) but I told my nurses I couldn't take that again. The 'wound vac' was still experimental in 2002 but used frequently now.

It's what saved my arm from going to the trash as medical waste. When I woke up from my dressing change it was two days later and everyone was talking to me like I was two years old.

Nothing can prepare you for brain damage; my mentor had a stroke, ex Mr. Right Now fractured his skull doing street luge and was comatose for four days, (yes he was wearing a helmet) a girlfriend had a brain tumor removed and another girlfriend was in a horrid car wreck. They all told me what it was like, how different they felt, what their symptoms were. Thought I got it but only very abstractly, it turns out. A functioning mind can't comprehend brain damage, there's no point of reference. Suicidal thoughts were weird because of the timing. They started at year three and were over by year five. (So please wait, with life there's hope.) What kept me from suicide is my parents. It broke their hearts when I was injured, I couldn't do it to them. I'm glad I'm still alive and having new experiences.

Email, alisa@PBSurvivors.org

Bendt Sornson / Pagosa Spring, Colorado, USA

I started my adventure in photography during my senior year in high school and met Alisa about a year after graduation—early 1983. She was one of the first models that I was able to shoot with. Alisa was also one of the few at that time that was always ready to go do a shoot and always had confidence in my ability's and herself in front of the camera—it made shooting with her easy and fun.

We lost touch for a few years and then reunited out in Los Angeles in 1987, while I was working for a studio in Hollywood. (Halloween was a big adventure. Limo's and Twinkies). After I moved from L.A. back to

Minneapolis we lost touch again. When I re-found her, it was well after her burn. I had done a Google search for her and found out basically what had happened through one of the Stunt Actors websites and then found a link to PBSurvivors.org. We talked on the phone after that and I was able to visit her out in Portland while traveling.

I can't say that this was not a shock after she told me what had happened. I honestly had no idea what to expect when we met again in Portland. I have never personally known anyone who has had to go through what she (and the others I met via PBS) did—and continue to go through. It was great to see Alisa again. It was also humbling and encouraging seeing the strength that she and the other survivors I've met have.

Betsy Pucci-Stemple / Minneapolis, Minnesota, USA

I am smart and kind of pretty. I have big boobs. I have been told that when I drink Tequila, it is both terrifying and hilarious to be near me. I can be a good friend and listener. Also an epic bitch. I love to eat but hate to cook and I am powerless against blue corn chips. I wish I could speak French. The following things have been said of me "Betsy  once caught a falling star which she keeps in her pocket everywhere she goes, and she knows how to eat soup with chopsticks."

Chris Backer / Halifax, Nova Scotia, Canada

My two year "burniversary" is almost here and I am a survivor. I'm the vice chair of The Maritimers Unite for Medical Marijuana Society, I produce my own pot-cast. *The Maritime Medical Marijuana Show.* I'm on the board of the Canadian Burn Survivors Society and I run Karma Compassion Society where I advocate for medical marijuana patients.

I would like to take my experiences and share them that others may learn from them. Life goes on, for me and for you. Living after a tragedy isn't always a choice, sometimes it just happens. Surviving is what happens once you realize you're still alive.

PLAHS (peaceloveandhippyshit)

Email, chrisbbacker@hotmail.com

Epilogue

In 2011, PBS's managing director Mike Yas and I were trolling for grants; trying to ease financial burdens for fellow survivors. Turns out getting grant's to distribute as cash is tough, getting grant's for 'things' is easier. Encountering red tape, I remembered the fun I had creating that silly, pill bottle collage. Art is a great therapeutic tool, a soothing meditative practice and a positive, constructive way to release negativity. Mike and I adjusted our goals and were very happy to receive a grant for five grand last November to create 'Art.'

We figured an anthology would include most people and thought it would be lovely to embrace Canada and the United Kingdom to get different perspectives. (Example: socialized medicine vs. privatized insurance . . . can we have a third choice?). We also wanted to include friends and family members, burns take so long to heal, everyone is affected.

I met Nancy and Yolonda in 2003 at The WBC, or The World Burn Congress, run by The Phoenix Society. 'Firefighter's Quest for Burn Survivors' a charity in Glendale, CA sent us. It was in Cleveland that year, it moves around the country. Being surrounded by hundreds of people who got it, didn't need explanations, people who weren't afraid or grossed out, was more than helpful, it was downright cheerful. Quest sends a pack of LA peeps yearly and I always looked forward to meeting up with everyone. The WBC is a lovely four day party / convention that has been going off for twenty five years. The Phoenix Society is organized and tries to be inclusive, offering freebies to first timers. Attendance is around eight hundred people.

Los Angeles is lonely when you're not working. I moved to Portland in '06. Finally done with surgeries, I wanted to be near family and my brother and his wife live in Lake Oswego. (Right below Portland.)

I was dismayed to find there were no Burn Charities in Oregon! 'How does everyone get to the WBC?' I asked at the monthly meeting in Oregon's only burn unit. Crickets. Everyone looked around the table. 'What's the WBC?' It was heart breaking. Maybe that's why we had such a hard time securing a grant, no one here had ever heard of 'burn support.' Portland Burn Survivors, Inc. started in 2009 with Mona Krueger as our managing director. (I need one, brain damage has left me with permanent short term memory loss). Mona left to write her book and co-author Bethany's in 2011 and Mike took over.

If you've been thinking about it, I recommend starting a non-profit; getting off the ground takes a year (for the IRS to give a 501c3) and cost's a grand (robbery, haha.) But once you get past that little yukkedy yuk, you are free to fundraise. Your corporation doesn't have to do taxes unless you've made more than $25,000. (And if you make that much, you can afford an accountant.) PBSurvivors has never even come close; we check a box on an electronic post card and email it to the IRS. . . Super easy and you'll be pleasantly surprised at the fun you can have on a wee budget.

The PBSurvivors.org website helped AnnMarie and Sara find us this past year (2013). Sara is the newest survivor among us, burned this past February. AnnMarie was burned as a child and being from a small town, never knew another burn survivor. I'm so happy they connected. Everyone who participated I've met personally except the Britt's.

The English contingent that joined *"...do I believe?" stories and art by survivors* I met on Facebook; hopefully we can meet in person one day. Absolutely adore you all. Social Media is a great way to find each other. A Canadian Survivor facilitates a good Facebook group, 'Burn Victim Survivors' with over seventeen hundred people, queries get answered fast.

People that have been through life altering injuries, their close friends and family, are all in a secret club, only the initiated need apply. From the outside looking in, people see pain and loss but often miss the clarity-love combo; it's powerful, insightful and draws us together.

(Brain damage also has a secret club but we can't quite remember, when do we meet, where's the convention and what's that secret handshake again?)

Thank you to everyone who participated in PBS's Art project. Thanks for your bravery and honesty and thank you too for all the laughs along the way; burn survivors are sublime at gallows humor.

Portland Burn Survivors Inc's mission: 'To help burn survivors live happy, rewarding lives; for burn survivors, their friends and family.'

And you don't have to be from Oregon. That's just our address.

Xox~adc